all you need is less

all you need is less

The Eco-Friendly Guide to Guilt-Free Green Living and Stress-Free Simplicity

Madeleine Somerville

Foreword by Billee Sharp

Published in the United States by Viva Editions, an imprint of Cleis Press, Inc.,
2246 Sixth Street, Berkeley, California 94710.

Printed in the United States.
Cover design: Scott Idleman/Blink
Cover photograph: iStockphoto
Text design: Frank Wiedemann

First Edition.
10 9 8 7 6 5 4 3 2 1

Trade paper ISBN: 978-1-936740-79-6
E-book ISBN: 978-1-936740-91-8

Library of Congress Cataloging-in-Publication Data

Somerville, Madeleine.
All you need is less : the eco-friendly guide to guilt-free green living and stress-free simplicity/ Madeleine Somerville. -- First edition.
pages cm
Includes bibliographical references and index.
ISBN 978-1-936740-79-6 (trade paper : alkaline paper) -- ISBN 978-1-936740-91-8 (ebook)
1. Sustainable living--Handbooks, manuals, etc. 2. Green products--Handbooks, manuals, etc. 3. Urban homesteading--Handbooks, manuals, etc. 4. Thriftiness--Handbooks, manuals, etc. I. Title.
GE196.S66 2014
640.28'6--dc23

2014001445

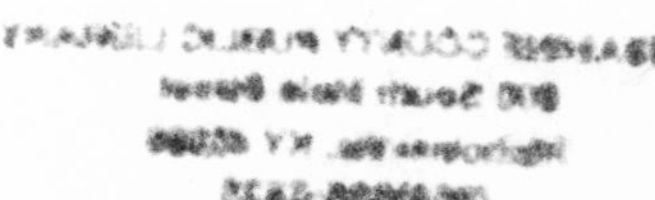

For Adam, and for Olive

Indubitably.

CONTENTS

FOREWORD BY BILLEE SHARP xiii

INTRODUCTION xv

(Or alternately: PANIC! Your home is filled with toxic waste!) xv

The characters in this book xvii

CHAPTER 1: HOME 1

The ugly duckling of the environmental movement 1

The cost of consumption 4

Shopping secondhand 8

Make it 13

Laundry detergent 13

Alternatives to dryer sheets 15

All-purpose cleaner 20

Tub scrub 21

Soap scum remover 22

Hands-free silver polish 23

Floor cleaner 26

Hardwood floor polish 28

Window spray 29

Floor duster 29

Stainless-steel appliance cleaner 31

Stainless-steel pots and pans polish 33

A word about plastic 34

CHAPTER 2: BODY 39

Basic hygiene boot camp 39

Choosing cosmetics 43

Make it 46

Eye makeup remover 46

Moisturizer 47

Whipped body oil 49

Natural microdermabrasion 49

Simple body scrubs 50

Shampoo and conditioner 53

Toothpaste 57

Deodorant 59

Toner 60

Meringue mask 60

Lady time 61

Hair removal 65

Shaving cream 67

Depilatory cream 68

Waxing 68

CHAPTER 3: LIFESTYLE 71

Being green is good for the waistline 71

Home, sweet home 74

Why *Beg, Barter, Borrow* should be the new *Eat, Pray, Love* 79

How to remember your reusable bags 85

Addictions 88
Make it 91
Clothesline 91
Rain barrel 95

CHAPTER 4: FOOD AND DRINK 99
Eating simply 99
Reducing waste in the grocery store 102
Taking on take-out 105
Make it 110
Punch-yourself-in-the-face salsa 111
Delicious tzatziki 112
Zero-electricity, cold brewed, basically-the-solution-to-global-warming coffee 113
All about organics 115
Boho table settings 120
Simple food storage 123

CHAPTER 5: GARDENING 127
A word from the gardening guru imposter 127
Make it 129
Herb garden 129
Salad garden 131
Real live vegetable garden 132
Raised garden beds 138
A pesticide-free garden 141
Seed storing 143

Start composting 145
Worm compost 146
Weed killer 150
Weed barrier 152

CHAPTER 6: RELATIONSHIPS 155
What to do when your partner is a soul-sucking planet killer 155
Quiz: are you an insufferable enviro-nag? 160
Be gentle with yourself 163
How living green can save your relationship 166
Good gifts 170
Make it 174
Personal lubricant 174
Massage oil 176

CHAPTER 7: HEALTH & WELLNESS 179
Apple cider vinegar cures everything 179
Alternative therapies 181
How (and why) to stick a small ceramic teapot up your nose 184
Make it 186
Magic tea for cold and flu season 186
Epsom salt aromatherapy bath 189

CHAPTER 8: BABY 193
Welcoming your adorable little waste machine 193
Why Craigslist should be your baby's middle name 196
Toys, toys, toys 201

Keep it neutral 205
Poop 207
Cloth diapers 210
Baby skin care 214
Make it 215
- Belly butter 215
- Baby wipes 218
- Disposable wipes 219
- Cloth wipes 220
- Baby-wipe solution 221
- Diaper rash cream 223

CHAPTER 9: PET 225

Your dog does not need a sweater (or a stroller) (or boots) 225
Make it 228
- Stinky dog spray 228
- Pet bed 228
- Flea spray 230
- Pet toothpaste 230

Litter box tips for sexy cat ladies 231
Shedding 232
The litter box 234
Make it 236
- DIY newspaper kitty litter 236
- DIY wheat litter 238

General litter box tips 239

CHAPTER 10: HOLIDAYS 241
How to curb holiday excess without becoming a Scrooge 241
Make it 245
Wrapping paper 245
Recycled paper gift bow 247
Make a difference 249

CONCLUSION 255
(Or: Time to Pony Up, Freeloaders) 255

ACKNOWLEDGEMENTS 259

NOTES 261

ABOUT THE AUTHOR 263

INDEX 264

FOREWORD

LESS IS MORE

The great hope for the twenty-first century is that humankind will find the vision and the intellectual resources to alleviate the suffering and damage that our industrial technology continues to bring to our planet and species. As our environmental problems become more apparent to more people there will be something of a second chance for those paying attention. Sadly, it is a popular lament that individuals feel daunted and diminished by the vast problems that we face. Green initiatives undertaken by states, municipalities, and individuals reach out into the population, but still, the overall picture seems grim: we have a long way to go to remedy the issues.

It is difficult to address such a huge and important topic without coming across as depressive, bossy, and pedantic; consequently, many shy away from facing the harsh truths and becoming part of the global solution. Understandably, enviromentalism has become the elephant in the room in contemporary society: the tenets of green living are at odds with the ethos of consumerism. Nevertheless, many of us understand that for human life to continue here we have to address sustainability. Often, the small gestures we make, such as avoiding throwaway coffee cups or plastic food containers, seem ridiculously miniscule and redundant in the face of the dominant mainstream trends. Then one considers the seabirds, dolphins, and whales who are dying daily with their gullets stuffed with plastic debris.

It is a hard, horrible, and frightening reality to face, and one can't help but wonder why so many of us choose to turn our faces to the wall and ignore the biggest problem that has ever beset our species.

Lucky for us that some proponents of green living have an upbeat attitude and a sense of earthy humor.

When I sat down to read Madeleine Somerville's *All You Need Is Less*, I was ready to glean a few extra tips on how to negotiate modern life in the greenest way possible. I was not disappointed, as Somerville is thorough in her desire to live an ecologically sound existence, and there is not an area of household management that she hasn't considered. Any reader, however green-conscious, will find some new angles to adopt in these chapters, but there is more. Somerville understands the difficulties of making lifestyle changes; she realizes that often there is ideological and logistical resistance; and, she offers the reader valid pointers, explanations, and arguments for making greener choices.

All You Need Is Less continues a valuable tradition of inspirational green literature, but unlike so many others, Somerville employs her own enthusiastic humorous energy to make her writing a lot more enjoyable than many other offerings. I believe that her light style, propensity for optimism, and a good laugh will bring many more of us to the realization that we can turn an unthinking culture around to create a sustainable lifestyle on our beautiful green planet!

Billee Sharp
Author of *Lemons and Lavender: The Eco Guide to Better Homekeeping*

INTRODUCTION

(OR ALTERNATELY: PANIC! YOUR HOME IS FILLED WITH TOXIC WASTE!)

This is the way most eco-friendly books start—right? Terror-inducing lists of the carcinogenic chemicals you are liberally slathering all over every single surface in your house, painting you as an unwitting eco-villain, happily Lysoling your way straight to Hades.

Well, lady, you can just relax and unpack your bags—we won't be going on any guilt trips today.

I'm not going to go on at great length about the chemicals in our cleaners or the monsters in our makeup; many fabulous books by people far more intelligent than I have already worn down that road (and also it sounds like a lot of work). At this point I think we all know that cleaning with bleach is bad and soda cans should go into the recycling. We're beyond that, yes?

What we're going to talk about is how to go about realistically adopting an eco-friendly lifestyle without losing your mind from the soul-destroying guilt of using a plastic bag because you forgot your reusable ones in the trunk of your car (*again*), *or* becoming a preachy know-it-all whom everyone loathes from the tips of her organically shampooed hair to the toes of her naturally sourced recycled sandals.

I mean it's all gotten kind of complicated, hasn't it? These days you're not "green" enough unless you quit your day job and devote your entire life to attaining an entirely carbon-neutral lifestyle, or throw out all your possessions and replace them with their new "green" alternatives.

Guys, I don't want to give up my fridge for a year. I don't want to become a self-righteous soapbox preacher standing on a street corner shouting, "I can smell your fabric softener from here, HUSSY!" And I definitely don't want to have to take a reference book with me to the cosmetics department—choosing a perfect shade of pink lipstick is hard enough without spending twenty-five minutes cross-referencing each individual ingredient until finally breaking down into exasperated sobs beneath a shelf full of loofahs.

This whole eco-friendly thing seems to have devolved into a horrific cycle of guilt, shaming, and one-upping, and as a result people are becoming annoyed and exhausted. We are living in a world where one of my grocery bags says "This reusable bag makes me better than you," and I am kind of starting to believe it.

It doesn't have to be this way. It *is* possible to take easy baby steps toward a more earth-friendly lifestyle without stress, guilt, or judgy eco-shaming.

I think it's important to tell you that I'm not an expert, and I think that's kind of the point. I haven't traded in my car for a bike, nor do I intend to. I live a fairly normal life with a slightly insane husband, a ginormous dog, and the most beautiful baby I've ever seen.

Within the scope of this fairly normal life I also do weird things like shampoo my hair with baking soda and clean my fridge with olive oil, and these things are small enough and simple enough that anyone could do them, if they wanted to.

The only hard part is beginning, which is where this book comes in.

In this book I will share my crazy hippie ways with you, and although they are designed to shift you toward a more eco-friendly existence, I promise that once you've turned the last page you won't feel guilty, and you won't feel overwhelmed. You won't feel superior, and you *definitely* won't ever have to stand bewildered under blinking fluorescent lights in the laundry aisle trying to choose between "spring breeze" and "fresh cotton" scent ever, ever again. And isn't that reason enough right there?

THE CHARACTERS IN THIS BOOK

You know when you read a juicy memoir and in the preface it says something to the effect of, "Names and identifying characteristics have been changed to protect the identity of those involved"?

I'm not doing that. While this definitely isn't a sordid tell-all (sorry), I do include some personal anecdotes about my husband, our daughter, and our dog, because I think that reading about how to stop the earth from killing us all is significantly more fun if you can have a good laugh (at other people's expense) while doing so.

The reason I haven't changed their names or their identities is because what is the point of *finally* getting a book published if you can't use it as a platform to publically ridicule your husband?

Exactly.

So, given this information, I thought it might be worthwhile to offer a quick introduction to these characters, so that you know whom I'm referring to when I reference their names in later chapters.

Adam

My husband.

Six-foot-two, hazel eyes, and facial hair that occasionally reaches a Zach Galifianakis level of beardedness.

It would please Adam no end if I said that he was the inspiration for this book, and in some ways it wouldn't be entirely untrue if I did.

Although I am the self-proclaimed hippie in the relationship and Adam isn't what you would call an "environmentalist," and he doesn't ever "recycle" or "walk" or even "think about Mother Nature," he has still managed to teach me a few things about eco-friendly living.

He taught me that reusing can be cute by proving that a shiny new sports car has nothing on a dude driving a busted old minivan. He taught me that recycling can be kind of gross, by wearing his underpants until they were little more than a bunch of holes attached to a waistband. Above all, however, he taught me the importance of reducing, by kindly zipping his lips whenever I started blathering on about a crazy new eco-friendly initiative I wanted to try.

This being said, the dude is crazy. He once lured me into our bedroom with a trail of chocolate and then jumped out from behind the door wearing a stocking mask. The worst part is I wasn't even that surprised—in our house, Adam trying to trap and terrify me using assorted confectionaries as bait is just called "Tuesday."

So, while he has taught me a lot (including more than I ever needed to know about twerking) and been remarkably encouraging during this journey toward a more earth-friendly lifestyle, the real credit for this whole endeavor needs to go to our big puppy, Gus.

Gus

My dog.

When we first brought this big clumsy English Mastiff puppy home, I was still cleaning with a popular anti-bacterial liquid, one that had a poison warning label on the bottle. I loved how well it worked, and the strong, fresh smell it gave our home (which provided undeniable proof that I had cleaned). But that first night with Gus, as we sat on the kitchen floor petting him and marveling over his paws—four sizes too large for his body—I watched him flop down and start licking the floors I had mopped with that toxic cleaner mere hours before.

That's when I knew things had to change. I knew I needed to find an alternative to that fluorescent cleaner, for little Gus's sake.

Five years later my enthusiasm for products that are gentle on the earth and my family has grown almost as much as Gus, who is still chubby and cute, but at almost 200 lbs. can definitely no longer be called "little."

While he has been significantly demoted with the birth of our real baby, Olive, I will forever have him to thank for inspiring my lifelong love affair with borax and baking soda.

Olive

My daughter.

The writing and publication of this book occurred almost simultaneously with the pregnancy and birth of our daughter, Olive, and here's a Pro Tip for anyone else contemplating hatching both a book *and* a baby at the same time: Ohmygod, why? No really, *why*? Are you crazy? No! Don't do that!

Also: coffee!

Olive has quickly become the love of my life, and I am physically incapable of talking about her without becoming a simpering sentimentalist, but clichéd, flowery sentiments be damned, she makes me want to leave the world in better condition than I found it.

Having a child has further driven home the need for us to take action to preserve and restore the earth for the next generation, because as the saying goes, we do not inherit the earth from our ancestors; we borrow it from our children.

Furthermore, I don't want to be *that guy*, the one who asks nicely to borrow something and then returns it stained and damaged, clogged with oil and bald from overuse. *Especially* if I'm borrowing that thing from a baby. (Seriously, what kind of jerk do you have to be to rip off a *baby*?)

This book was written because I strongly believe that we owe it to our children to consider the impact of our actions on the world they will grow up in, the world that they will in turn leave to their children, and I will do anything that I can to help make that world a better place.

(If that heaping dose of guilt doesn't motivate you, consider that our children will be the ones making the decision to stick us in a nice nursing home—or in the one featured on last week's *60 Minutes*.)

Me

Me!

I have a B.A. in sociology and have spent the past five years as a Youth Resource Worker at a teen drop-in center. When I wasn't wrangling sassy teenagers, I was writing for our local newspaper or on my blog, and also making appearances at craft fairs and farmers markets, where the first tiny inklings of this book appeared in pamphlet form.

I am passionate about environmentally friendly living, but mostly I am tired of looking like a crazy person for all the weird stuff that I do.

This book is an attempt to lure you over to the green side because there's strength in numbers. The more of us using jars for coffee and hoarding aluminum foil, the better.

Finally, thank you so much for buying this book, or borrowing it from the library, or even just idly flipping through these pages in the cramped aisle of a bookstore while you wait for your friend to pick up her latest vampire shame-read.

I hope that you can find some wisdom in my words, and create a space in your life for these small changes. They do add up.

Namaste (just kidding),
Madeleine

CHAPTER 1
Home

THE UGLY DUCKLING OF THE ENVIRONMENTAL MOVEMENT

The way the green movement has picked up steam in the past five years and entered mainstream culture seems as if it would be an environmentalist's dream come true.

No longer are you regarded as strange for recycling, the neighbors have stopped whispering about that pile of vegetable scraps you keep in a box in your backyard, and in some areas you may even be able to talk about rain barrels and carbon footprints without so much as a batted eyelash. This, my friends, is progress! I can almost see Al Gore smiling from here.

But, wait! It's not all blue skies and Birkenstocks. Something strange has happened along this long-awaited journey to mainstream acceptance.

Somewhere between the advent of curbside recycling and the use (and abuse) of the term "upcycling," the three R's have been whittled down to two. So whereas *reusing* has never been trendier (patchwork scarves made out of old sweaters, anyone?), and *recycling* has been embraced by even the most recalcitrant, *reducing*—the ugly duckling of the environmental movement—has been strangely absent from the conversation.

In an era when environmentalism has become increasingly trendy, this concept has been almost entirely skipped over, and it's not hard to understand why: nothing is more antithetical to our consumer culture than the idea of simply *not consuming*.

You can't sell reducing on Etsy, you can't show off your commitment to the concept with a trendy bumper sticker or cool water bottle—because the whole point is to not buy superfluous bumper stickers or water bottles in the first place.

This means that while pop culture is dancing around loudly proclaiming "Green is the new black!" the concept of reducing anything has been entirely abandoned.

It's ironic, really, because the ability to reduce is perhaps the most important aspect of any environmental movement: reducing conspicuous consumption, reducing useless *stuff*, reducing your waste, and eventually, as a result of these endeavors, being able to reduce the amount of time you spend shopping, cleaning, and organizing your possessions.

The fact that this concept is being so studiously ignored, however, suggests something even more dangerous than our obsession with consumer culture—it hints at the faddishness of the "Go Green" movement. If environmentalism becomes just another trend like neon or tie-dye, if it is represented purely by the items we're buying this season instead of the fundamental changes we make to how we think, act, and behave, we run the very real risk of seeing "Recycling" on the wrong side of one of those ubiquitous "Hot or Not" lists in a few years' time.

Wait! Don't go anywhere! I know that I've gone all Debbie Downer on you, but I'm working up to the upside of this whole shebang. And there is an upside, a huge, wonderful upside. Here it is: embracing the concept of reducing takes the least effort of all the environmental changes you can adopt. It's almost Zen in its simplicity (call it the Tao of the Lazy Environmentalist) because, in order to reduce, you spend a lot of time *not* doing.

Not researching. Not buying. Not reusing. Not recycling.

Why? Because there's nothing to research, buy, or find creative ways to dispose of. You stopped the process before it started by deciding you didn't need it in the first place—whether "it" was another pair of flip flops or a new car.

Keeping the decision to reduce at the forefront of your brain means you don't have to drive yourself insane comparing and contrasting eight different brands of fabric softener that claim to be eco-friendly, wading through the green washing and the jargon for hours before giving up and drowning your sorrows in a box of wine. You simply wash your hands of the entire thing and make the decision not to purchase fabric softener at all.

It is also important to popularize the concept of reducing because the effort needed to become environmentally friendly, while not huge, is simply not worth it for many people. We human beings are an inherently lazy species, programmed to take the path of least resistance every single time (and if you doubt this, allow me to present as evidence: the Snuggie, the Clapper, and the Lap Bowl).

So, while the amount of effort needed to rinse an aluminum can, sort it into the appropriate recycling bin, and take it to the recycling depot isn't huge, if you're not at least a tiny bit passionate about environmentalism the chances of this happening are pretty slim. Why? Because it's still harder than doing nothing at all.

This is where lobbying local government for innovations to make eco-friendly living easier comes into play. Curbside recycling and composting programs make choosing eco-friendly options that much easier and thus more likely to happen. But this laziness and inertia is also where that wily third R can truly shine.

In terms of the effort one needs to expend in order to earn positive karmic points from Mother Nature, choosing to reduce will always give you the most bang for your buck. It's basically the Snuggie of the environmental movement.

So hop into its warm embrace, choose to do nothing, and feel good about being a lazy environmentalist. They're the best kind.

THE COST OF CONSUMPTION

With shopping being one of the most popular leisure activities in North America, buying things goes without notice most of the time—so much so, that an international movement, Buy Nothing Day, was started to curb this habit and draw attention to its almost-involuntary nature.

Despite their popularity, however, possessions aren't

treats; they are needy little demons that suck your time, your money, and also probably your sanity if you have too many of them. (In this respect, they're not unlike children.)

As soon as you assume their ownership you become responsible for their well-being for the entirety of their lives, start to finish. You must find a place for them in your home, take care of them, clean them, pay to have them fixed when they break, and then dispose of them properly when they have outlived their purpose. (OK, so maybe in this last respect they are kind of different from children. Guys, you can't just dispose of children when they have outlived their purpose. Yes, really. No, not even when they behave like needy little demons—which is always, obviously.)

I believe that it is precisely because we look at belongings as treats or rewards that we forget that they are in fact, responsibilities. So we keep treating ourselves and rewarding ourselves and all these treats and rewards pile up and up and up until we find ourselves stressed and overwhelmed and in the strange position of having to buy even *more* stuff in order to organize, and store all the first stuff.

The home organization industry has exploded in the past decade, and not because everyone suddenly decided to clean up their act and have tidy shoe closets. It's because we own more possessions than ever before.

We all love to be savvy shoppers and bargain hunters, but no matter how much of a deal you think you're getting, you need to remember that buying things costs more than the dollar amount on the price tag. It costs square footage in your home and time in your day spent on cleaning and maintenance. It costs someone's time to repair it if it breaks, and unfortunately almost everything ultimately ends up costing space in a landfill when the thrill wears off.

Becoming more conscious about what you are buying, and conscious too about how you will store, clean, maintain and dispose of each separate item you put into your shopping cart can go a long way toward tempering the amount of stuff you consume, not only because you will be aware of the implications of each purchase, but because it's so annoying that it might just put you off shopping altogether.

Seriously, having to mentally run through something's life cycle before you hand over your hard-earned cash to buy it is so depressing and exhausting that I rarely end up making the purchase at all.

For example: Picture me in early spring, realizing I need some sunglasses. It's finally sunny and I have emerged into the light, blinking and squinting like a mole-person. Late at night I stand in front of the mirror examining the onslaught of new wrinkles crowding the outer corners of my eyes and—*lord yes,* do I need sunglasses!

So, a-shopping we will go. The next day I stand in front of a display packed with cute styles with fun plastic frames, and I start the ridiculous process of imagining purchasing a pair for ten dollars. They are nice, but super-basic and probably uncomfortable, and the lenses have no protective coating and will most likely scratch almost right away. Because they are only ten dollars, I probably won't be obsessively careful with them, and if Gus doesn't sit on them I'll most likely end up leaving them on a bus after a day at the beach.

The bus driver will find them and maybe even try them on before deciding that the bright turquoise frames do nothing for his coloring, then throw them in the garbage.

The sunglasses will probably snap under the weight of a dozen other trash bags en route to the landfill (burning fossil fuels all the way, naturally), and while pecking through mountains of garbage a cormorant, attracted by the bright color of the frames, will attempt to eat and subsequently choke on one of the arms and die. DIE!

Reader, I do not buy the sunglasses. Instead, I construct a sunhat out of recycled aluminum foil.

See? Reducing *and* recycling—how fun!

In all seriousness though, doing this before heading to the cash register can help you cast off the yoke of consumerism you wear heavily around your neck, help you stop buying plastic bins to organize your stuff, and result in your just *having less stuff* altogether.

So, before you buy something, try and imagine the life cycle of this item: How will you pay for it? Where will you put it? How much time will it take to clean it and maintain it? What will happen to it once you can't use it anymore?

And then once you are flummoxed and exhausted by all those questions, maybe, just *maybe,* don't buy it (for the cormorant's sake, if nothing else).

SHOPPING SECONDHAND

While I am obviously a big fan of minimizing the sheer amount of excessive *stuff* we bring into our lives, I am well aware that we can't all live monastic existences with nothing to our names but a bowl and a spork. (And honestly, I wouldn't want to. Sporks concern me. I don't want my utensils to be able to multitask better than I can, thank you very much.)

Even if you do manage to cut out buying all the plastic junk that you don't need and the impulse purchases that will break in a week, even without all that noise, you will still need to buy something, at some point. It's pretty much unavoidable. This is where shopping secondhand comes into play.

It took me a while to come around to the idea of buying someone's castoffs. Initially, the idea of literally walking a mile in someone else's shoes seemed repugnant, and it was difficult to find the patience to wait the sometimes months it took to find the right piece of vintage furniture.

As time went on, however, I realized that buying secondhand is the absolute best way not only to save some cash, but to make sure that you're getting a quality product too.

Let's think about this in terms of clothing first. You know those stores that offer shoes for ten dollars, or shirts for five? I can almost guarantee that you're not going to ever see any of those items in a decent secondhand store.

While they look amazing new, there's a reason that they're so cheap.

Here's what happens: You're walking along one fine spring day, perhaps sipping coffee from a pickle jar, when you pass a sweet pair of leopard-print ballet flats in a store window. You think to yourself, "Erhmagherd! Adorable leopard print flats for only ten bucks? Sold!" You skip to the cash register, happily fork over a tenner, and you and your sweet new kicks live happily ever after.

For about two months.

Then the toes get scuffed and the finish starts wearing off, and you can't even use leather cleaner to restore them because they're not leather, they're some sort of weird PVC plastic deal. The sole starts separating from the shoe, your toes poke through, and eventually they're so unsightly that you have to throw them out entirely.

Not such a good deal anymore.

When you buy secondhand, however, you are seeing the item as it looks after weeks, months, or sometimes years of use. You can pretty much guarantee that the condition in which you find the item is roughly the condition in which it will remain—whether it's a shirt, a couch, or, yes, a pair of shoes.

Secondhand stores are like crystal balls that you can use to look into an item's future and see how it stands the test of time.

Time is a cruel mistress, especially to goods that are made poorly using cheap materials, and in this way the junk gets weeded out of secondhand stores pretty quickly.

I am particularly a fan of buying secondhand furniture, because it tends to be a big-ticket purchase for many people. Searching for a design-friendly item that fits within a tiny budget often leads us straight to big-box stores with inexpensive "starter" furniture. And look, I'm not judging, I did it too. But next time, before you fall in love with the picture in a catalog and find yourself heading straight to the store, cash in hand, head to your computer instead and do a quick search through your favorite online classified site.

Go ahead and type in the name of that perfect $499 couch to see what turns up. Do this even if you have absolutely zero intent of buying it secondhand.

What you will most likely find, especially with the more popular big-box stores, is a handful of ads posted by people trying to sell this very same item after owning it for just a year or two. The ads will have pictures attached, and these pictures will be your crystal ball into a future filed with sagging cushions, faded upholstery, and chipped particleboard legs.

THAT is what your couch will look like, my friend. Not the nice, brand-new, immaculately styled catalog photo, but THAT.

Obviously, no one *wants* to buy crappy furniture. I think that given the choice we would pretty much *all* opt for something of good quality—we're talking real wood, durable upholstery, eco-friendly design. Unfortunately when you find furniture that fits these criteria, you will also usually find that it costs three or four times what you can afford to pay—long live champagne tastes and beer budgets!

The solution? Rather than bankrupting yourself in pursuit of magazine-worthy décor or filling your place with a string of cheap, poorly made furniture, buy secondhand. Shopping the classifieds instead of the showroom allows you to save at least 50 percent of what it would cost to buy new, and you can see exactly how that item stands up to normal wear and tear, as well as extend its life cycle.

The downside to shopping secondhand, and I suspect the reason a lot of people don't do it, is that you have to be patient. We are very much an instant gratification society. We are used to getting exactly what we want, when we want it, and not a second later, but when shopping secondhand you kind of have to lurk and stalk and peruse. It can sometimes take months before you find what you're looking for, and in the interim your friends and coworkers will mock you behind your back and start referring to you as "the crazy Craigslist lady."

This was the case with our couch. Oh god, the couch.

Here's the deal: Pre-husband and pre-dog, I owned a cream-colored sofa and two white armchairs. They were comfortable and beautiful, pristine and perfect.

After adding Adam (he of the Doritos-handprints) and Gus (a mammoth, drooling, shedding, fart factory), the color of my furniture could best be described as greige. And not in a trendy "new neutral" way either, but in a dirty, gross, this-is-why-we-don't-have-nice-things way.

I loved that furniture, but I guess I loved my husband and my dog more or something, because the time came when I knew it was time to say goodbye. I sold the pieces on our local Facebook buy and sell group (shedding a single tear as I saw them driving away in the back of a stranger's pickup truck), and the hunt began.

I lurked on Craigslist for weeks while our living room stood empty. We sat on the floor as I clicked through ad after ad, searching for something I couldn't even put a name to; "I'll know it when I see it" was all I could manage to mumble feverishly when Adam asked (repeatedly, in increasingly shrill tones) what, exactly, I was looking for while we used throw cushions as seats.

And look, while this story has a happy ending, I'm not going to pretend that shopping secondhand goes without heartbreak. Twice I convinced Adam that I had found it—The Couch. We would arrange a meeting time, fight over directions and arrive sweaty and panicked an hour late, only to find that the couch looked nothing like the picture or had generous grease marks polka-dotting the seat cushions.

After the third such excursion Adam had had enough and he staged a mutiny. “No more!” he fumed. “I’m done!”

This type of endeavor is not for the faint of heart, and Adam had clearly proven himself too weak to continue, so I had no choice. Undeterred, I pushed onwards.

I’m glad I did, because shortly thereafter I found it, the one I’d been waiting for! It was infinitely better than I could have imagined, in immaculate condition with clean lines and slim legs and soft tufted gray upholstery. I was in love. This was it!

My adrenaline surged. I contacted the seller and made him promise to hold it until I could come see it. There was only one more obstacle in my path: Adam.

Because I am a *lady*, but also because I know that his mom will be reading this book, I’m not going to say what kind of shady deal I had to make in order for him to agree to help me pick it up, but I will say this: it was *totally* worth it.

The moral of this long-winded rambling tangential story? Buy second-hand. You’ll get better quality for less money, and it might just pay off for your partner too.

MAKE IT

We sacrifice a lot when we ask our cleaners to eat through dirt and grime while we hardly lift a finger. The same chemicals that promise to do all the dirty work for you can also irritate your hands, cause breathing difficulties, and be potentially fatal if ingested—kind of a crappy trade-off just to avoid some elbow grease.

If you are willing to put some muscle into it, you can reap the rewards of a full wallet, a clean house, *and* a spotless conscience to boot.

Here are a few recipes to get you started.

Laundry detergent

1 bar soap, grated

1 cup washing soda

1 cup borax

1 cup baking soda (optional)

Don't be intimidated, kittens! If you can operate a cheese grater and a measuring cup, you CAN do this.

First of all, go to the grocery store and wander over to the laundry aisle. Note how you can smell the overpowering scents of "Fresh Breeze" and "Spring Meadow" even through their SEALED containers. Gross.

By now most of us are aware that most store-bought laundry detergents use chemically derived fragrances and harmful chemical compounds to coat the fabric that we wear closest to our skin. This is bullshit (and overpriced bullshit at that).

Stride purposefully past all those brightly colored, expensive plastic bottles of chemical goo and look along the bottom shelf—that's usually where the good stuff is stashed. We're talking about the stuff with no advertising budget, no marketing strategy, just pure product. (Does it sound like I'm talking about cocaine? I'm getting a bit of a coke-vibe here. We're still talking about laundry detergent, just to be clear.)

You're going to buy one box of washing soda (different from baking soda), and one box of borax. Note how they are packaged in easily recycled cardboard boxes as opposed to hulking plastic bottles.

Pay for your purchases (probably a grand total of ten dollars or less, unless you caved and bought a chocolate bar at the checkout, which, I mean, no judgment here).

Now we need some natural soap. If there's someone in your community who makes soap, it's great to make the choice to support them, if not, see if you can find a brand called Dr. Bronner's at your local health food store, or order it online.

If you live in a backwater where no one makes soap and your local Piggly-Wiggly doesn't stock Dr. Bronner's, don't despair! You can use Sunlight soap or any bar soap, really. It won't be quite as natural or eco-friendly but it'll do the job.

So buy a bar of whichever soap you're using, pop it in the freezer for a few hours so it hardens, then grate it. If you're fancy you can use a food processor, I use one of the fine sides of my cheese grater.

When the soap is grated, add it to one cup of borax and

one cup of washing soda. You can add a cup of baking soda for extra deodorizing, or omit it for a stronger detergent.

Mix well.

You're done!

Use 1–2 tablespoons per load. This detergent is great in cold water and is low-suds, making it a great choice for front loader and HE (High Efficiency) washers too.

Alternatives to dryer sheets

If you thought I got excited about laundry detergents, wait till you hear me pontificate about dryer sheets!

People, we are paying good money, money that could be better spent on a package of fine goat cheese, for a product that basically just coats your clothes with perfumed animal fat.

Perfumed. Animal. Fat.

This is crazy, right? Am I the only one who finds this crazy?

Happily, this is one situation where we can practice being a Lazy Environmentalist: simply doing nothing and buying nothing is a fantastic solution to this problem. Stop using dryer sheets altogether, and you've solved the problem with less effort and energy than it took to create it in the first place.

Many times you'll find that you didn't even need the sheets in the first place and don't miss them one bit. But here are some trouble-shooting tips if you do in fact find yourself longing for those stinky little lard napkins.

Problem: Help! Help! My laundry is all staticky and stuck together!

Solution: Lady, calm down. You are frying your clothes. (Or alternately: Dude, calm down, you are frying your clothes. I offer this alternate phrasing because I have heard that men sometimes do laundry. I am taking this at face value, because I have never personally witnessed such goings-on in my house.)

The most common reason clothes get staticky is because you've run your dryer too long and every last morsel of moisture has been blasted from the fabric. Thus, your poor cardigans have had no choice but to cling desperately to your attractive argyle work socks for fear of spontaneous combustion.

One way to solve this problem is to run your dryer for less time, or on a damp-dry cycle. This will not only solve your static problems and be far gentler on your clothes, it will save you money too, because dryers are one of the most inefficient and energy-sucking household appliances out there.

If you want to take it one step further, many people are opting to ditch the dryer altogether, which I can assure you is much less work than it sounds. On a sunny or windy day, laundry can dry in as little as thirty minutes, and looks awfully picturesque while doing so.

Indoor drying racks are also a great option during the winter, or if, like me, you live in a colder climate where "summer" means two weeks of unholy heat dropped into the middle of three months of rain. (You can turn to page 91 for more info on line-drying your clothes.)

Any way you choose to do it, though, avoiding the dryer will eliminate static, save money and energy, and help your clothing look newer, longer.

> **Problem:** But I like my clothing to smell like a Fresh Spring Breeze™.

> **Solution:** Well the obvious remedy here is to hang your clothing outside, you know, in an *actual* fresh spring breeze, but I think we both know that's not what you mean. You miss that certain *something* that scented dryer sheets provide, non?

Essential oils are your friend here. Find a scent you like (lavender and citrus are my favorites) and add a few drops to a damp cloth before tossing it in the dryer.

It'll add a subtle scent to your clothes without the toxic chemical stews.

> **Problem:** My clothes aren't as fluffy as they were before.

> **Solution:** Balls! No, not that kind!

Dryer balls do a fantastic job of fluffing clothing, reducing static, and decreasing drying time. They have become more popular in recent years, but unfortunately the popular versions that are sold in many stores are often made of PVC plastic.

Rather than tossing plastic balls in with your clothing, a better option is eco-friendly and naturally fire-retardant dryer balls made from 100 percent wool.

These are incredibly easy to make, and would make a fantastic activity for school-aged children. See the sidebar on page 19 for simple instructions.

For ultimate smug-hippie bragging rights, you can go through your closet or the racks at your local thrift store to find a sweater made from 100 percent wool. By unraveling the sweater and using its yarn to make the balls, you have achieved the ever-coveted hippie triumvirate: reducing, reusing, *and* recycling. You get all the points!

If sitting around making wool balls isn't your jam, don't despair. This is a great chance to support an independent artisan by searching around and ordering a few from www.Etsy.com (an online marketplace for independent crafters and artisans worldwide). Just type "dryer balls" into the search engine.

Whether you're buying them or making them, wool dryer balls reduce static while fluffing your clothes—and if you want scent you can add a few drops of essential oils directly onto the ball.

I've used these for four years now as well as making them to sell at farmers markets, and I always got positive feedback. Generally, I use between two and four balls depending on the size of the load.

HOW TO MAKE WOOL DRYER BALLS

MATERIALS:

100 percent wool (look for something recommended for felting)

hot water

pantyhose

small crochet hook (size 3–5mm)

Take your wool and wind it tightly around two fingers until it is the size of a ping pong ball.

Remove the ball from your fingers and continue wrapping the wool tightly around itself until it reaches the size of a small mandarin orange. Cut the wool and draw the end through the middle of the ball using your small crochet hook.

Take the ball and tie it inside of the pantyhose, separating multiple balls with a knot. Toss it in with your laundry the next time you do a hot water wash, or soak it for five to ten minutes in a bowl of boiling water.

After washing, run it through the dryer until it's dry to the touch. Take it out of the pantyhose and continue wrapping it until it reaches the size of a tennis ball, and then draw the end of the wool into the middle of the ball again.

Repeat the whole hot water-pantyhose-dryer process again, then just keep your balls in the dryer and live happily ever after, dryer-sheet free.

All-purpose cleaner

This is a fantastic all-purpose cleaner with some anti-bacterial properties too.

I know that some cleaning sprays advertise that they kill 99.99 percent of bacteria. Without delving into the effectiveness of antibacterial cleaners or the increased resistance of viruses as a result of their overuse, I will simply note that, according to one study, simple white vinegar was 90 percent effective against mold and also 99.9 percent effective against bacteria,[1] with the added bonus of not potentially killing you if you happen to drink it.

Just sayin'.

If you have an old spray bottle kicking around, give it a thorough wash and then fill it with hot water, leaving two to three inches for the rest of the ingredients.

Add to the bottle:

3 tbsp. white vinegar

2 tbsp. Dr. Bronner's liquid Castile soap

1 tbsp. borax

Mix until the borax is dissolved, then get trigger happy!

I use this for wiping down countertops, tables, windowsills and pretty much all other general cleaning tasks around the house.

If you use scented Castile soap, it's nice aromatherapy too.

Tub scrub

Do you guys remember that commercial for a popular cleaning spray that featured cartoon bubbles peeping on a naked woman as she showered? Yeah, that just about sums up my feelings about all those spray-on foam cleansers promising a sparkling bathroom with zero effort. Gross.

It takes a big toxic wallop to duplicate the effects of a good scrubbing, and, for the good of your biceps and Mother Earth, it's probably better to just stick to the real thing.

Plus, I can pretty much guarantee that you'll never need to worry about your scrub brush objectifying you while you are just trying to shave your damn legs.

For this simple tub scrub, you'll need just three things:

¼ cup baking soda

1 tbsp. Dr. Bronner's Castile soap (or natural dish soap)

Warm water

Mix the baking soda and soap together and slowly add warm water until you have a thick paste. Scoop some up with a sponge or non-scratch abrasive pad, then roll up your sleeves and get scrubbing.

The baking soda does an incredible job of cutting through soap scum, and the soap makes surfaces shiny and clean.

After you've scrub-a-dub-dubbed, rinse the rub with warm water, step back, and admire the shine.

Soap scum remover

This is for everyone living with a glass shower door that has somehow become opaque with soap scum buildup—those of you that want to fix this issue, that is. I mean, if you are still dealing with residual trauma from the peeping-bubbles situation, and kind of appreciate the extra privacy that a few layers of hard-water buildup provide, fair enough.

If, on the other hand, you want to get back to putting on impromptu shower dance routines for your partner while he brushes his teeth (what? just me?), you are only three short steps away from achieving this goal.

First, find yourself a clean, empty spray bottle and some trusty ole white vinegar. If you can get your hands on pickling vinegar it might work a bit faster because it has a slightly higher acetic acid content, but if not, your run-of-the-mill white vinegar will work fine.

Using a microwave or saucepan, heat the vinegar. (If you use your microwave, you'll be multitasking by cleaning and deodorizing the microwave too! Just wipe off your microwave's interior with a soft cloth after you're done.)

Carefully transfer the hot vinegar into your spray bottle (a funnel is helpful), and, using the bottle's finest mist setting, lightly spray the entire shower door. The goal is to use a really fine mist so that the vinegar sticks to the surface instead of dripping off.

Leave the whole situation to soak for fifteen to twenty minutes, then wipe with a clean cloth or a non-scratch abrasive pad.

Depending on how crusty your doors are, you may have to repeat the process a few times, but in the end your shower doors will be looking crystal clear once again. (You'd best start practicing your dance moves!)

Hands-free silver polish

This tip might have limited application, because no one in my generation seems to own good silver. Or maybe I've just been hanging out with the wrong people.

You know what, that's probably it. There's probably a whole subset of late-twenty-somethings who are swanning around eating delicious things with delicate silver utensils, and meanwhile I've been using stainless steel hand-me-downs like a *chump*.

I am kicking myself for not seeing this sooner.

At least my parents had their priorities straight. We owned a beat-up old GMC Safari van, and I don't think my youngest sister ever saw clothing with the tags still attached until she could buy them with her own money, but damned if we didn't have a whole dresser full of good silver. Now that I've discovered the existence of this Secret Silver Society, I'm glad they did, but as a child the task of polishing said silverware often fell to me, and so I loathed it with every fiber of my being.

This chore took forever, required painstaking attention to detail, and meant breaking out a bottle of stinky silver polish that literally had a skull and crossbones on it. I can't even count how many paper towels I burned through polishing that stupid silver, not to mention the brain cells I lost from inhaling the noxious fumes.

(This is something I like to bring up with my parents occasionally, just so that they know I still hold them accountable for all that lost potential.)

A few years ago, however, everything changed. My dad showed me a method of cleaning silver that was not only quick but also super-effective without causing loss of more precious brain cells. After trying it myself, I knew immediately that I had to spread the word.

I might not be able to go back in time and liberate my past self from this drudgery, but if I can save just one other innocent child from the elaborate inlay of a heavily tarnished soup tureen, I will have done my job.

This method truly is amazing and works on any piece of genuine silver that can be fully immersed in water (jewelry, utensils, etc.). But don't use it on anything with accents of leather or bone.

MATERIALS

Boiling water
Plastic bin
Baking soda
Aluminum foil
Tongs
Clean, soft cloth

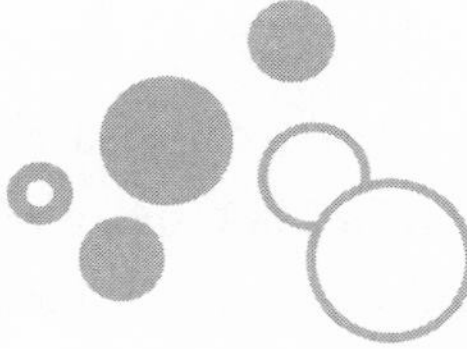

While you are waiting for your water to boil, find yourself a plastic container big enough to completely submerge whatever you would like to clean. Completely line the bottom of the bin with aluminum foil (shiny side up).

When the water boils, immediately pour it into the container and add roughly one tablespoon of baking soda for every four cups of water. Immerse the silver and wait. After a few moments some wondrous bubbling and fizzing will occur and you may be able to literally see the tarnish being drawn out of the piece and onto the aluminum foil.

At this point I usually find it helpful to raise my hands above my head and shriek excitedly as though I have performed a small miracle (which, if you consider the facts, *I kind of have*). (Don't skip this step. I'm convinced that it helps.)

Give the silver a few more minutes to soak after the fizzing action has stopped, and then use your tongs to remove it from the bin. Once it has cooled, give it a good wipe with a soft cloth to remove any remaining tarnish.

Badly tarnished items may need to go through the process several times, so just replace the aluminum foil and baking soda, and add fresh boiling water each time.

You're welcome, children.

QUICK TIP

A little cooking oil can go a long way to silencing squeaky hinges in a pinch. Just dab a bit onto the offending hardware with a rag and open and close the door a few times to work it in. Repeat until the squeak is gone.

Floor cleaner

You're not going to like this, but honestly, the best way to clean your floors is to put on some rubber gloves, get down on your hands and knees with a bucket of soapy water, and just start scrubbing. There's nothing that will clean your floors as well as this, plain and simple.

Despite knowing this, I rarely do it. Free time is scarce around these parts, as I'm sure it is on your end, and when I do manage to find a free half hour or so, why would I want to spend it on my hands and knees scrubbing floors when I could be doing far more important things like catching up on celebrity gossip or tweezing my eyebrows?

Exactly.

That's why this recipe exists. It always tides me over until I get around to doing it the old fashioned way every few months or so.

(By the way, scrubbing floors can be incredibly cathartic, and an *excellent* way to release pent-up rage. You can conduct angry, breathless one-sided arguments as you scrub, and nothing makes floors shine better than a heaping helping of righteous indignation.)

SUPPLIES

Sponge mop
Dish soap/Dr. Bronner's liquid Castile soap
Vinegar
Microfiber cloth
Elastic band

DIRECTIONS

Fill a large bucket or sink with hot water, and add one tablespoon of dish soap or Dr. Bronner's Castile soap, and one cup of vinegar.

First, sweep or vacuum the floor thoroughly to get rid of dog hair, crumbs, and the like. Then start mopping. If your floor is quite dirty (no judgment here), you'll need to change out your water a few times or you'll just be spreading dirt around.

After you've finished mopping, wring out your mop and, using the elastic band, secure the microfiber cloth over the mop head. Then go over your floor again with the mop, using the microfiber cloth to dry the floor. This eliminates streaks and also speeds up the drying process.

QUICK TIP

If you don't have time for a full mopping, just pop the microfiber cloth on your mop head, dampen it slightly and spill some vinegar on your floor. Give it a quick go-round; the vinegar will both clean and deodorize. This won't offer any sort of really deep cleaning but will tidy things up a bit until you can get down to business.

Hardwood floor polish

This is the best way I've ever found to clean and polish real hardwood floors, and all it involves is a little black tea.

In a saucepan, boil 4–6 cups of water. Add four black teabags, turn off the heat and let the tea steep for 5–10 minutes. When the tea has cooled, use it to mop your hardwood floors. You can either transfer it into a spray bottle or use it right out of a mop bucket.

The slight acidity of black tea helps lift dirt off the floor, and the color disguises any nicks or scratches.

No need to rinse.

Window spray

Next to the floor polish above, this is the easiest thing in this whole book. It's almost embarrassing to have to write it out, but it's a great alternative to that magic blue liquid, so I have to share it.

It also works wonderfully on surfaces like microwaves, faucets, mirrors, etc.

OK. Here goes.

1. Combine equal parts white vinegar and water.
2. Spray onto your surface and wipe clean with a soft cloth or newspaper.

-Fin-

Floor duster

In the past few years, single-use cleaning products have proliferated at a disheartening and bewildering pace. There is just no good reason to be throwing out paper towels, dusting cloths, and floor mop pads when there are things that work just as well—if not better—right under our noses.

Having said that, I do understand the appeal. It's annoying to haul the vacuum out just for a quick job, and while brooms are great for dirt and crumbs, pet hair and dust often end up swirling around in midair, sneakily giving the appearance of cleanliness until it all settles again in five minutes. Then, if you're anything like me, you are left protesting "I swear I *just* swept!" while the socks of your guests gradually acquire the look of angora.

Gus is a prolific shedder, to the point where I am utterly convinced that he

is a magical bottomless pit of hair. I swear I could brush him for days, and the fur would keep flying and filling bag after bag, and nowhere would I ever even begin to see a glimpse of the end. I love animals, but pet hair drives me crazy, and I have sort of made it my mission to minimize the amount flying around my house, so while you will always know I have a dog (he's kind of hard to miss, after all), you might just think I have a maid too.

Over the years I have discovered that a fabulous alternative to buying those one-time-use floor mop pads is outfitting your cleaning cupboard with five or ten microfiber cloths instead (they'll be getting dirty, so choose dark colors over light). Microfiber is a great material for trapping dust and hair as well as shining surfaces, and can even easily replace the disposable pads on popular floor sweepers.

To make a do-it-yourself dust mop without having to buy another cleaning tool, just use elastic bands to secure a microfiber cloth over the bristles of your broom, and go to town on those fur tumbleweeds.

If you have already purchased one of these popular floor sweepers, however, it's simple to hack it into being eco-friendly. Just cut a microfiber cloth to slightly overlap the mop pad, and then secure it into the little pinchy-holder things (I believe that is the technical term).

These cloths work just as well as those disposable pads—if not better—and instead of shelling out for new pads each week, you just shake them off outside, toss them in the washer and they'll soon be ready for another go-round.

(Madeleine: 1, Gus: 0)

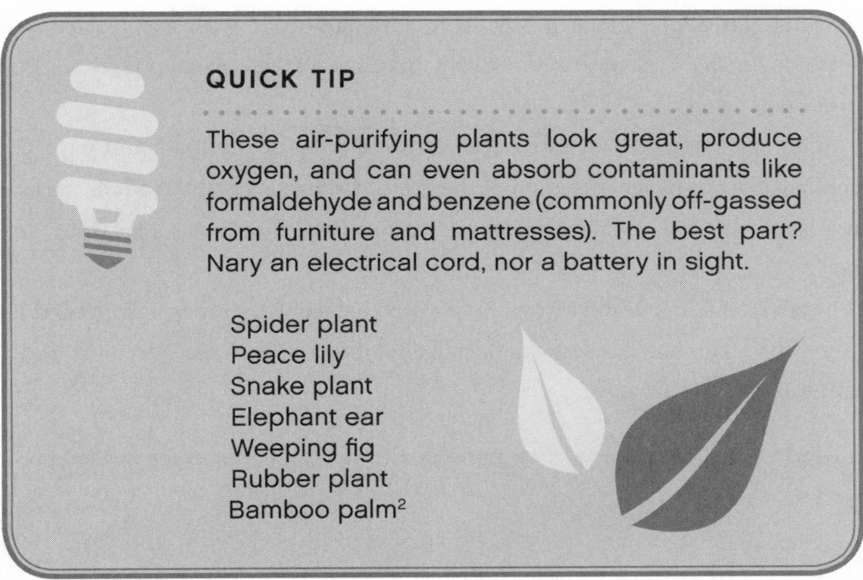

QUICK TIP

These air-purifying plants look great, produce oxygen, and can even absorb contaminants like formaldehyde and benzene (commonly off-gassed from furniture and mattresses). The best part? Nary an electrical cord, nor a battery in sight.

Spider plant
Peace lily
Snake plant
Elephant ear
Weeping fig
Rubber plant
Bamboo palm[2]

Stainless-steel appliance cleaner

Most stainless-steel polishes are made up of a cleaner that removes dirt and grime from appliance fronts, plus an oil base that gives sheen to the surface.

One-use cleaning products like this tend to be really expensive, and in this case manufacturers are probably relying on the fact that you already laid out thousands for your shiny new appliances, so you might be more inclined to shell out again for their upkeep. Luckily, it's really simple to replicate the effects of stainless-steel cleaners with the same brilliant results using simple dish soap and olive oil.

First grab a microfiber or other soft cloth dampened with soapy water, and wipe down the surface to remove any dirt, handprints, grease marks, or dog drool (ahem).

Dry the surface, then dab a little olive oil onto a fresh cloth and wipe the appliance down in the direction of the grain. Continue until the whole surface has been covered, then buff any excess until the stainless looks shiny and new.

Stand back and admire your handiwork before it becomes besmirched by your filthy partner/children/pets/self once more (approximately four and a half minutes from now).

QUICK TIP

If your toilet bowl has a nasty ring that won't disappear, grab some rubber gloves and a pumice stone. It may take a few minutes, but the pumice stone will gently take the ring off without using harsh chemicals or damaging the bowl's finish.

Stainless-steel pots and pans polish

For the longest time Adam and I cooked our meals in an old set of pots and pans that dated all the way back to his university days. Once we had eaten all the Teflon off the bottoms, however, we decided it was time to invest in a new set that had lids, functional handles, and 100 percent less flaky additives to our meals.

Our new stainless-steel pots were christened by me with boiling water to cook some veggie dogs—an appropriate beginning considering my culinary talents (or lack thereof).

Over the years I did manage to use them for a few more ambitious culinary endeavors, and along the way I discovered that cream of tartar works like a hot-damn to restore their shine when they become dull-looking.

It's the kind of simple solution that's right up my alley.

1. Wet a microfiber cloth, and sprinkle with cream of tartar.
2. Give the whole pot a thorough polish, inside and out.
3. Rinse well, and dry with a clean cloth.

This also works with stainless steel sinks and utensils. I find that my cutlery often starts to look cloudy over time, so every so often I fill a bucket with roughly eight cups of hot water and about one tablespoon of cream of tartar. I let everything soak until the water cools, and then polish with a microfiber cloth.

Everything looks gorgeous and shiny again in no time.

QUICK TIP

To clean smooth-top stoves, use a paste of baking soda and water. Gently scrub the stovetop with a soft cloth and the baking soda solution, then wipe and rinse thoroughly. Use a flat razor to get rid of any baked-on rings around the burners. A quick spray with a 50/50 vinegar/water combo will make it gleam.

A WORD ABOUT PLASTIC

Plastic can be great because it's cheap, but unfortunately it's also *cheap,* as in low-quality.

My grandmother was a terrific snob of great conviction whom we used to refer to as "She Who Must Be Obeyed." She was known for reducing my siblings and me to tears if we didn't pass the salad bowl in the right direction (and if you are asking yourself why it matters in the slightest in which direction a bowl full of spinach is passed, you have pretty much summed up my childhood).

She was a woman who, like many of our grandparents, knew the value of frugal living, but also of buying items of good quality. This is a woman who saved elastic bands and wax paper, but always shopped at the best clothing stores.

One of her favorite sayings was "Cheap is more expensive in the long run," and although I have never found proper directional-food-passing etiquette to be of much use in my daily life, I've found that she was bang-on with this particular piece of advice.

Generally speaking, it's helpful to think of plastic as equating with disposable. In some areas where you would never want to avail yourself of an indefinitely reusable alternative even if one existed—think dog-poop bags or dental floss—this works out fine, but when we're talking about objects that we will be using on a long-term daily basis, plastic just doesn't cut it.

Nine times out of ten, items made out of plastic will wear faster, break more easily, and require replacing sooner than their more expensive counterparts made of wood, glass, or metal.

I'm definitely guilty of being attracted to plastic because of its availability, trendy appeal, and low price, but over the past few years I've shifted my buying habits toward purchasing something of good quality that can be maintained, rather than buying something cheap that will soon break and have to be replaced.

This cycle of break-and-replace, buy-and-dispose-of-and-buy-again: this is what companies want. Marketing execs know all too well that we human beings are weak and, much like crows or monkeys, we are easily seduced by anything shiny and new. They are more than happy to satisfy these simple desires in the form of mass-produced plastic crap.

So how do we stop this vicious cycle? How do we demonstrate to those faceless corporations that we are better than crows and monkeys, *dammit?* Well first of all, before heading to the store to add to our collection of mass-produced baubles, we can ask ourselves, "Do I really need this?"

"Need" is the operative word here. It connotes necessity, something essential that cannot be done without. In this sense, no, I don't *need* a new pair of three-dollar flip flops to replace the eighteen pairs that have broken already. Nor do I *need* a new plastic juice jug because the old one was etched and cloudy-looking after just a few uses.

What I truly need here, my grandmother would be happy to advise me with a haughty sniff, is a pair of *good* shoes and a solid glass pitcher, both of which will be in use long after her acerbic tone fades from my memory.

We know how to fix wood, leather, glass, metal. These materials *can* be fixed, and what's more, it's *worth it* to fix them. We're fast losing our inclination to repair things in favor of buying new, and that is a pretty depressing concept to contemplate. So do my Grandmother's memory proud and avoid plastic whenever possible.

It would bring her great joy to know that so many people were obeying her.

QUICK TIP

Start hoarding.

This tip may seem strange, since everyone these days (me included) is all about simplicity and less! stuff! But the kind of hoarding I'm talking about doesn't involve eleventy-seven cats, or precarious piles of decades-old newspapers.

Instead, hoard like my grandmother did. We're so accustomed to single-use items that we often forget to save things like aluminum foil, jars, rubber bands, and zippered plastic bags for reuse. As long as it hasn't come into contact with raw meat or moldy food, you can give most things a quick wash with dish soap and they'll be ready for another go-round.

(Just don't blame me when your friends laugh at your stash of neatly folded wax paper remnants. And they will laugh. Trust me.)

CHAPTER 2

Body

BASIC HYGIENE BOOT CAMP (AND I MEAN REEEALLY BASIC)

It goes a little something like this: Use soap.

Oh, I know you are a clean person and you probably smell nice too. In fact, I have no doubt that your personal hygiene is beyond reproach.

But choosing to use plain old bar soap instead of that pump hand soap, body wash, shower gel, or super-expensive foaming, miracle-moisturizing mousse you got on sale can do wonders for your skin, your local landfill, and the crowded shelves of your shower caddy too.

People tell me that the reason they use body washes instead of soap is that soap is too drying or too harsh on their sensitive skin. With conventional bar soaps this is often true, and I mean, fair enough, no one likes walking around in a skin suit that feels two sizes too small. Nevertheless, I didn't usually have this experience and am a huge fan of natural bar soaps, so I wanted to find out why so many people were passing them over in favor of the plastic-packaged stuff.

Because I sometimes like to pretend that I am a girl detective like Nancy Drew, I hunted down some answers from my very own soap lady, Kirsten French of Be Clean Naturally. Kirsten was a regular at the farmers markets in my old hometown of Squamish, BC. Starting with soaps and gradually working her way into shaving creams, laundry detergents, and other personal care and home products, she always sought to use minimal packaging, offered product refills when possible, and had a real passion for getting clean the natural way. She helped me get to the bottom of The Case of the Natural Bar of Soap (aka, Why good-quality natural soap is actually better for your skin than anything found inside of a bottle and also, *Why do you have to be so lame, Madeleine?*)

"Typically, commercial soaps and shower gels are made from a detergent base, which strips the natural oils away from our skin, leaving us dry and scaly," French explained. "This causes many people to then slap on skin cream to combat the itchy, tight post-shower feeling. Detergents are very inexpensive to make and are derived through a laboratory process. They also have a lower pH than traditional soap, which means that they need synthetic chemicals, such as triclosan, added into them to make them antibacterial."

After briefly mocking me for pretending to be a girl detective, Ms. French went on to explain that triclosan is rapidly accumulating in our oceans and affecting the ability of whales to reproduce (save the whales!). And whereas shower gels are often laden with synthetic fragrances and preservatives that can be irritating to the skin, sinuses, and eyes, soap is inherently antibacterial without needing anything nasty added.

If I haven't convinced you yet, or bored you with my pro-soap tirade, other important points to ponder are the number of resources and amount of energy required to create these products. We have to mine or harvest the raw materials, make the plastic bottle, fill it with product, transport it, advertise it, recycle the bottle after the product is finished, mine resources to create another bottle, and on and on forever.

Beyond the environmental implications lies the fact that you're *paying* for every cent of that mining and producing and packaging and transportation, when you thought you were just buying some nice sudsy junk to put on your loofah.

So! Now that we've finished eviscerating all those shower gels, mousses, body washes, etc., let's take another look at our humble bar of natural soap.

No bottle to make or recycle. No triclosan or antibacterial chemicals washing down the drain jeopardizing the health of our oceans. (And the whales! Remember the whales?) Last but definitely not least, if you buy soap locally there's little to no transportation required, and some artisans (like our lovely Ms. French) even sell their bars of soap with absolutely no packaging—nothing to make, nothing to recycle, just a good old-fashioned bar of soap.

So how can you find one of these good, natural bars of soap? Your local farmers market, craft fair, or health food store are great resources, and you'll also be supporting small business owners in your own community. You're looking for something created with pure essential oils and ingredients you've heard of, like olive oil and other nutritious oils like almond, avocado, or jojoba.

If the ingredients aren't listed or you can't pronounce them, move on.

Bonus: Because natural soaps don't dry your skin as much, you may find that you don't need as much moisturizer, so you'll save money and resources there too. And if you genuinely do have sensitive skin that is prone to rashes or breakouts of eczema, it's even more important to avoid products loaded with additives that make them foam, chemically derived artificial fragrances to make them smell nice, and Oprah knows what else.

QUICK TIP

Ditching the shower gel and body wash also frees up a lot of shower space. Do you want to know what I have in my shower right now? A bar of soap, a razor, and two glass jars (we'll get to the reason for the jars in the next few pages). That's it. No poofs or loofahs, no bottles of shampoo or body wash, just those four simple items.

This setup drastically reduces the amount of time I have to spend in the shower, reduces shower-stall clutter, and makes it easier to clean when the time comes. I also like to think that the jars add an infuriating air of intrigue for bathroom snoops.

CHOOSING COSMETICS

Balancing one's need for luscious lashes with makeup's possible deleterious effects on the environment can seem like quite the quandary for an eco-conscious individual, but it's really much simpler than it appears.

As far as I can tell, there are three distinct options when considering how to look good while still doing right by Mother Nature—I find myself bouncing back and forth between them:

1. Go full-on hippie style: fresh-faced and makeup-free. (This always seems like a great idea until the fifth person I run into asks me why I look so tired/sick/pale and I have to start shrieking, "Guys! This is my face! This is just what my face looks like!")
2. Research and purchase exclusively products that claim to be environmentally friendly. This is usually my preferred option, but as with anything labeling itself eco-friendly these days, the process of wading through spurious claims and green-washing can be exhausting when all I want is to do is buy some lip gloss, *dammit!* Also, some (but definitely not all) eco-friendly products are simply not as effective as their conventionally made counterparts.
3. Buy the same old big-name beauty products you always have, Mother Nature be damned. (She should have thought about this before she saddled us with such short eyelashes and prominent under-eye circles.)

Each of these come with pros and cons, so we'll go through each one and you can decide which is right for you.

If you go with option 1, you are brave and you probably have amazing skin and I kind of hate you. (Um, I mean I *encourage* you! Go YOU!) If you're comfortable going *au naturel*, this is the best thing in the world for both your face and the environment. You get all the gold stars.

It's also worth mentioning that choosing to go makeup-free is a choice that can be more easily made by being healthier in other areas of your life too. A healthy lifestyle with plenty of fresh air, exercise, and nourishing food is reflected in the skin. The healthier you are inside, the healthier you'll *look* outside.

Adam would like me to add, for the benefit of partners everywhere, that according to one Scottish researcher, people who have sex at least three times a week look about ten years younger than their less libidinous counterparts.[3] So, hey! That's one idea for what to do with all that extra time you used to spend fussing with foundation and mascara.

I have a feeling, however, that most women will, at some point, want to use some cosmetics, even if just for a special occasion or to disguise a particularly angry pimple. So let's move on to option 2.

For option 2 we owe many thanks to the Internet. If you've got a few minutes to devote to the subject there's a wealth of resources out there to help you find products that are kind to the earth while simultaneously highlighting your cheekbones and bringing out your eyes.

One of my favorite resources is run by the Environmental Working Group, at www.CosmeticsDatabase.com. Using their exhaustive database of skin and beauty products, you can enter in the name of almost any cosmetic or personal care product and immediately have access to a full list of its ingredients. Not only that, but the Environmental Working Group provides each ingredient with a list of studies linking it to toxicity, cancer-causing agents, skin irritation, and more, rating the severity of each and rating the product from 1 to 10 based on how safe it is. You can also access best-of lists that will give you a rundown of the least toxic products in each category.

I find this website to be a great way to suss out the companies that are actually using environmentally friendly ingredients, as opposed to those that are just slapping a brown paper label onto a product and calling it "natural."

If this sounds like a good time, make yourself a cup of tea and get researching.

Now, option 3. If you aren't on board with avoiding makeup altogether (I hear you, sister), and you simply don't have the time or the desire to spend fifteen minutes meticulously researching environmental alternatives to your current beauty products, don't give up just yet.

It's true that you can't do much to change the products themselves or the ingredients used in their manufacture, and you're on your own for the effect they have on your body too, but there are still a few steps you can take to green your goods.

First, try to recycle all the product packaging that the item comes in, from the cardboard box to the plastic sleeve. Buy fewer but better-quality products to ensure you won't end up with a makeup drawer filled with stuff that doesn't live up to its promises. And finally, check out companies like Terracycle that offer recycling programs for things like mascara tubes and lotion bottles.

With locations in the United States and Canada, Terracycle offers the opportunity to recycle all sorts of unconventional items from flip flops to coffee pods—and in this case, used cosmetics. Head over to www.Terracycle.com if you lived through George Bush, or www.Terracycle.ca if you know what a toque is.

The site allows you to sign up for different recycling brigades free of charge, and, once you have collected enough of a particular recycling item, simply request a prepaid shipping label to send everything back to Terracycle for recycling.

The best part (other than actually being able to recycle toothpaste tubes instead of throwing them in the trash, that is), is that you earn one point for every item returned, and these points translate into real cash that you can spend on recycled products, or donate to a charity of your choice.

Now *that's* beautiful.

MAKE IT

Eye makeup remover

This recipe is as easy as pie, and it consists of one single ingredient: coconut oil.

Find a jar of unrefined, virgin coconut oil—usually found in the oil-and-vinegar aisle of most supermarkets—and massage a pea-sized amount onto eyelids and lashes.

Wipe clean with a soft, dry cloth, and boom! No more raccoon eyes! As an added bonus, coconut oil goes easy on that delicate under-eye skin and leaves it nicely moisturized too.

QUICK TIP

If you use coconut oil both for skin care and for cooking, purchase two separate jars, or divide the one you've got into two different containers. No one wants to find eyelashes in their stir-fries. (Probably.)

Moisturizer

I'm willing to bet that you currently own between four and six different kinds of body lotion. There's probably the giant one you got on sale at a big-bulk store, the travel-sized one you keep in your purse, some special cream for your hands and nails, and maybe a few gimmicky ones you got suckered into buying and now regret—you know, gradual tanning moisturizer, firming moisturizer, hair-growth-inhibiting moisturizer, magic unicorn pretty-lady moisturizer, etc., and so on.

To supplement and complement your body's own natural moisture, however, you don't need mass-produced lotions and potions. All you need are a few natural oils. The beauty of this tip really does lie in its simplicity.

By trading cream for oil, your skin will feel buttery smooth, your wallet will thank you, and your husband will never stop groping you even when you are *just trying to unload the dishwasher, Adam.*

It's been three years since I made this switch, and although it got off to a rocky start, I'll never go back.

See, when I first decided to forgo conventional lotions, I just walked down to my local health food store and picked up a bottle of sesame oil. Easy-peasy—right? Except the thing is, I didn't read the label properly and I bought toasted sesame oil, which—guys, please trust me, don't do this.

Toasted sesame oil is what they use in stir-fry. I love stir-fries and I make them all the time. Seriously, give me some bok choy, kale, and tofu, and we've got ourselves a party! But as much as I love a good stir-fry, I don't like *smelling* like a stir-fry. Since the very reason I had purchased eau de stir-fry in the first place was to become more eco-friendly, I couldn't very well just throw it out, could I?

So every day I faithfully rubbed myself down with that toasted sesame oil and, let me tell you, if you are looking for some space in your marriage this is the way to get it. I don't think Adam came within two feet of me for weeks.

So, yeah. In conclusion: just buy the normal stuff.

Sesame oil (the normal kind) and unrefined coconut oil are my favorite picks for moisturizers, but I've used almond and grapeseed oils with great success too.

Your skin is perfectly primed to absorb moisture after a bath or shower, so warm the oil in your hands and then take five minutes to work it well into your skin. Towel off any excess before getting dressed to avoid oil stains on clothing.

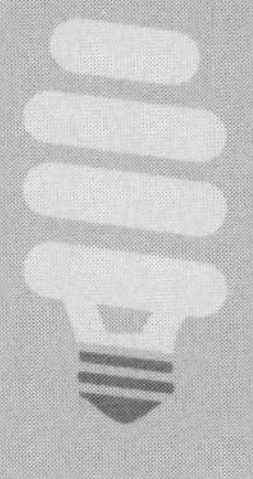

QUICK TIP

If you do drop some coconut oil on your shirt, or find yourself with some other sort of grease stain, try washing the stain with dish soap and letting it sit for five or ten minutes. Rinse and launder as usual.

Whipped body oil

If it feels too easy to just dig coconut oil out of a jar and slap it on your skin, or if you just like to feel a little bit fancy sometimes, this recipe is for you.

Put about a cup of coconut oil into a medium-sized bowl. Then, using a hand mixer and a whisk attachment, mix the oil until it reaches a soft, whipped cream-like consistency. The skin-smoothing effects are the same as the plain-Jane un-whipped oil, but it goes on a bit lighter and feels more luxurious.

Natural microdermabrasion

Microdermabrasion is typically a process whereby you pay hundreds of dollars for an aesthetician to sandblast your face with tiny particulates that slough off old dead skin cells and reveal a smooth new you. The recipe below employs the same basic idea, but costs pennies, takes seconds, and can be done at home.

I don't want to risk the ire of the FDA or the International Society of

Microdermabrasionists (if such a society exists, which I have no doubt it does) by going so far as to claim that this recipe will produce the same results as a professional treatment, but I *can* tell you that it's a fantastic and gentle exfoliant that works wonders on the sensitive skin of your face.

1. In a small bowl mix approximately 1 teaspoon of baking soda with a few drops of warm water—use just enough to form a thick slurry.
2. Gently (gently, now!) massage the paste into your skin with your fingertips. Baking soda is an awesome abrasive on its own, so you don't need to use much force, let it do the work.
3. After a few minutes of gentle massage, rinse your face thoroughly with lukewarm water and apply a gentle moisturizer.

I have found this to be a great weekly exfoliant for the face, and even that rough bumpy upper arm skin too.

(Ha! What? I don't have rough, bumpy upper arm skin!)

(Yes I do.)

Simple body scrubs

Once upon a time, I purchased a book of homemade beauty recipes. It was beautifully written, extensively researched, and illustrated with gorgeous hand-drawn pictures. I loved reading it and, what's more, I loved being *seen*

reading it. I loved the idea of sitting there all, "Oh hey it's me, Madeleine! Just relaxing in a park on a sunny spring day, reading about how to whip up my own fair-trade organic gluten-free citrus-mollusk brightening salve!"

I had high hopes for this book. With this book, I would be *that* girl. The one with the skin so fabulous and glow-y that everyone would be clamoring to know what products I used, at which point I would smile shyly before humbly admitting that my moisturizer was just a little something I had whipped up myself. People would ooh and aah, I'd get paraded around on someone's shoulders and damn, probably even get a medal or something.

Ask me if that ever happened.

I never made even one *single* recipe from that book's prettily laid-out pages. Not for lack of trying either. The problem was that each recipe listed at *least* five to ten ingredients, most of which were difficult to find and expensive to purchase when I did.

For this reason, simple beauty recipes (three easy-to-source ingredients or fewer) are more my speed, and body scrubs fit particularly well into this philosophy because the formula is so basic.

1 gentle abrasive + 1 oil/binding substance + some optional fancy extras = gorgeous silky-smooth skin.

Gentle abrasives include things like brown sugar, baking soda, coffee grounds, etc., and binding substances are what keeps the abrasives sticking together while you scrub. Binding substances can be oils like coconut or sesame, as well as things like honey. Optional extras add a little zing in the form of fragrance or appearance—stuff like spices, essential oils, or flower petals (oh, LA!).

Here are a few of my favorite simple scrubs. To make them, just combine all the ingredients, mix well, and store in a glass jar:

COCONUT BROWN SUGAR SCRUB (MY PERSONAL FAVORITE)

1 cup brown sugar
3 tbsp. melted coconut oil
Dash of cinnamon and cloves (optional)

WAKE UP! SCRUB

½ cup coffee grounds
½ cup fine sea salt
1–2 tbsp. olive, almond, or sesame oil

BRIGHT LEMON SCRUB

½ cup of sugar or fine salt
2 tablespoons lemon juice
1 tablespoon olive oil

SWEET SCRUB

¼ cup honey
2 tablespoons white sugar

Feel free to mess around with the measurements to get a scrub that's as thick or thin as you like, or go rogue with ingredients to create your own exfoliating scrubs. They're simple to make and easy to customize to the needs of your own skin.

Most importantly, however, when someone asks you how you got that silky-smooth, dewy looking skin, remember to smile and tell them that it was just a little something you whipped up yourself—didn't take five minutes!

Then wait for the parade to begin.

Shampoo and conditioner

I'm going to be honest and say that I usually lose people with this one, and I totally understand why. If someone had suggested to me four years ago that I wash my hair with the same ingredients you use to clear a clogged drain, I would have been shooting them some serious side-eye too. But, here we are, and that's exactly what I'm suggesting you do.

It's been three years since I stopped buying shampoo and conditioner, and I swear I haven't turned into a filthy, greasy hippie-troll person. If anything, my hair is better than it was before. (Seriously. I promise. Go look at my author photograph.)

I implore you to try, just TRY, the following recipe and see what you think. The process is dead-simple, ingredients cost less than a fancy coffee, and, really, you have nothing to lose. Here goes:

SHAMPOO

1 cup warm water
1 tablespoon baking soda

Stir well until the baking soda has dissolved, then pour over wet hair. Massage the mixture into your hair, paying special attention to the scalp. If you tend to have greasy hair, concentrate your efforts around the hairline and at the crown of the head as these are the oiliest areas.

If you have long or thick hair, feel free to double or triple the recipe; just keep the ratio the same.

When you're done scrubbing, thoroughly rinse your hair.

CONDITIONER

1 cup warm water
1–2 tablespoons apple cider vinegar (ACV)

Mix both ingredients and pour over freshly shampooed and rinsed hair. Massage into your scalp and leave for a few moments before rinsing.

Use 1 tablespoon ACV if you have oily hair, 2 tablespoons if it leans toward the dry side.

It's amazing how well these two simple ingredients work to clean and condition your hair. You save an incredible amount of money and you won't start your days by coating your head in nasties like sodium lauryl sulfate and artificial fragrances, both of which can be toxic and are commonly found in most shampoos and conditioners.

You also won't be buying and throwing away all those plastic shampoo and conditioner bottles, which kind of makes it worth it right there.

I always get a million questions when I tell people that I do this ("You wash your hair with WHAT?"). Here are the most common:

Frequently asked questions about this whole crazy shebang

Q: Is this for real?
A: Yes! Guys, I swear I'm not messing with you.

Q: Does it work?
A: Yes. Incredibly well. My hair is clean and healthy, and my hairdresser always remarks on how little damage there is and how smooth my hair shafts are (that's what she said!).

Q: Do you stink like vinegar?
A: OK, here's the thing. When you're rinsing, yes, it smells like vinegar: *it's vinegar.* But vinegar doesn't smell when it's dry, so no, I don't stink. Not of vinegar anyway. I mean if you were burying your nose in my head after a gentle spring rainfall, you might be able to smell it, but otherwise, no.

Q: Do you have lots of tangles? I'm worried my hair will be a rat's nest without conditioner.
A: NO. None. I can brush my hair straight through right after the shower and it is smooth-going and tangle free.

Trust me, whatever you are thinking, I thought it too. I know it sounds weird but it's amazing, and it *works*.

A few tips

If you're having a tough time getting past the vinegar smell, try popping a few cinnamon sticks or a vanilla bean in your bottle of apple cider vinegar for a few days before using it.

You could definitely make this mix in advance and store it in your shower, but because it's mostly water, you will be pouring ice-cold liquid over your head come shower time. This is extremely unpleasant (ask me how I know). As such, I usually recommend using a permanent marker to mark the 1 cup level on a few pretty glass jars to keep in your shower, then when it comes time to shower you simply measure out the baking soda and ACV and then use shower water to fill the jars to the right level. (Finally, the reason for the two jars in my shower, revealed!)

Feel free to tinker with the amounts of ACV, adding more or less as required. If your ends are a bit dry after heat styling, try smoothing them with a bit of coconut or olive oil.

Toothpaste

This toothpaste is super-simple to make, and my teeth have never felt cleaner or looked shinier—they're almost glossy! It's incredible.

This toothpaste will probably taste saltier than what you're using now, but it doesn't come in a plastic tube and also doesn't have any strange, potentially harmful ingredients. Definitely worth a try in my book.

INGREDIENTS

⅔ cup baking soda

½ teaspoon fine sea salt

1–2 teaspoons peppermint extract, or 10–15 drops peppermint essential oil

water

Mix all the ingredients together in a small glass jar, adding the peppermint oil/extract a little at a time to taste, then add water until you get a thin paste.

To use, either wet your toothbrush and use the bristles to scoop some paste out of the jar, or use a small spoon to apply a pea-sized amount to your brush.

When I started using this recipe I was worried that the baking soda would be too abrasive and wear away my tooth enamel or ruin my gold tooth or something, but then I did some sleuthing and discovered (thank you, Internet) that baking soda is actually *lower* on something fancy called the "Relative Dentin Abrasiveness Scale" than every single other toothpaste out there.

The scale runs from 0 to 200, with baking soda clocking in at a measly 7, while the closest commercial toothpaste comes in at 35.[4]

Also notable is that this is probably the first time Googling something actually made me feel *less* worried, instead of more. Usually I start off by searching something innocuous like, "Why is my leg so itchy?" (because dang, sometimes a lady just has to know), only to find myself three hours later, hyperventilating and in tears because I have diagnosed myself with an incurable leg-eating disease caused by a rare strain of German fire ants that Adam picked up on a trip to Europe as a teenager and has been incubating on his person ever since, until last Wednesday that is, when they hatched and attacked me in the night, and ugh, seriously, Adam—fire ants? *You would!*

I must admit that it did take me a while to get used to the saltiness of this recipe, but I couldn't get over how great my teeth felt, and now I find that using normal toothpaste tastes oddly sweet—like I'm brushing my teeth with frosting. If you're also having a tough time getting past the salty taste you can always omit the salt altogether, or change out the peppermint oil/extract for orange, cinnamon, or whatever rocks your world.

If you're not up for DIY toothpaste, another option is to consider switching your regular toothpaste to a natural brand free of horrific junk like sodium lauryl sulfate, preservatives, and artificial colors and flavors. You'll still get the benefits of natural tooth cleaners, and when you're done with the tube you can recycle it through a wonderful program called Terracycle. (More info about Terracycle on pages 45–46.)

Deodorant

If you don't like being stinky, but you also don't like slathering store-bought deodorants with questionable ingredients like aluminum right next to your breast tissue every day (and men, you have breast tissue too), you can either buy natural deodorants or make your own.

One of my friends used to rub a crystal under her arms instead of using deodorant and, guys, I think I'm pretty out there sometimes with this stuff, but I'm not THAT out there.

My recipe is simple and will have you smelling fresh all day long. Well, actually, because this is fragrance-free, you won't smell like anything, really. But that includes sweat. You won't smell like sweat! And it involves exactly zero crystals, so there's that.

COMBINE:

2 tablespoons coconut oil

2 tablespoons baking soda

2 tablespoons arrowroot powder (can usually be found in health food stores)

½ teaspoon melted coconut oil

Mush the first three ingredients together with your fingertips until they form a paste, adding ½ teaspoon melted coconut oil to help everything mix together.

Store in an airtight container, and massage a pea sized amount into each armpit in the morning, or as needed.

Toner

This recipe utilizes one of the great loves of my life, apple cider vinegar (or as I like to call it, ACV—we're tight like that).

Many people assume—incorrectly—that vinegar will be irritating to skin, but it's actually quite the opposite. ACV neutralizes pH and softens skin, and if the smell doesn't bother you it'll become one of your most-loved beauty fixes. (For more ACV love, turn to pages 179–181.)

To create a skin-soothing facial toner, just mix 50/50 water and ACV, and use a cotton ball or soft cloth to swipe gently over a clean face.

Meringue mask

It is truly one of the most delightful things in the world to apply a face mask, wait for it to gradually harden, and then stare at your immobilized features in the bathroom mirror and imagine you've had Botox. In fact, this describes most of my Saturday nights from ages fourteen to sixteen. (It was an awkward time. But I had great skin!)

This simple homemade mask tightens pores and leaves your skin feeling fresh and clean. I like to do it once a week or so, and it can easily be used for up to three people.

Ingredients
1 egg white
½ teaspoon fresh lemon juice

Beat the egg white until it forms stiff peaks. Then slowly stir in ½ teaspoon of lemon juice and whisk well to combine. Generously apply the mixture to your face, wait until the mask has hardened, then rinse with warm water.

Beautiful.

LADY TIME

All right dudes, we're going to be talking about menstruation. If you're cool with that, read on. If not, skip ahead and rejoin the party on page 65.

Very few women are overjoyed to have their periods, no matter what that stupid commercial says. It can be messy and inconvenient and also *expensive* because every single month finds us at the cash register buying tampons and pads (and, if stereotypes are to be believed, buckets of ice cream and crazy lady pills to make sure we don't turn into raging beasts).

I would be a lying crazy person if I said that I thought periods were awesome, but I also don't think they are the worst thing ever. I was interested to learn that, in some cultures, like Canadian First Nations, the menstrual cycle is considered to be a powerful cleansing ritual.

In some Canadian First Nations communities menstruating women aren't allowed to participate in sweat lodge ceremonies, but not because they are thought to be impure or unclean—actually quite the opposite. Sweat lodge ceremonies are thought to renew and cleanse the spirit, but women having their periods are understood to be undergoing a natural purification and renewal ritual from within. Thus, participating in a sweat lodge ceremony as well would be sort of redundant, and some believe that a woman's power is considered to be so great during this time that it may actually pull purifying energy away from others.[5]

How do you like that? I mean, if you want to get all deep about it, our periods aren't just an annoyance or an impediment to wearing white pants, but one of our strongest connections to the natural world.

But, hippie-dippy stuff aside, all this power and strength is of little help when you're shelling out for pads and tampons every month, and it also does little to soften the irony of the fact that our closest tie to the natural world also contributes to a significant chunk of its pollution. Pads and tampons have to go somewhere when we flush or throw them out, and with almost half of the world menstruating every month, there really has to be a better way to go about this.

So let's talk options.

First up, let me say that if you're going to try to go the natural route with menstrual products, you're probably going to come into contact with some blood. I know, and I'm sorry, but it's just going to happen. Let's not be grossed out, OK? These are our bodies, it's a normal event, and almost every woman out there has gone through this or will go through this at some time in her life, so let's get over the ick factor.

This doesn't mean that we're going to be painting with it or anything (and besides, that's already been done), but just be aware that we're not dealing with that neutral blue liquid they use in commercials, and that's OK. We are *women.*

If you're a tampon user, one option to consider is something like the Diva Cup or Moon Cup. These are basically little silicone cups that are inserted into the vagina to catch menstrual blood. Your vaginal walls form a natural seal with the cup so leakage is pretty much nonexistent—similar to what you'd find with using a tampon. But—and this is why I wrote the caveat above—when it comes time to change it, you will be removing a little cup full of menstrual blood.

You will have to take it out, dump the contents and then rinse it, and if this is going to make you whisper "Ohgodohgodohgod" before passing out face first onto the floor of a public restroom, it might not be the right option for you.

Know your limitations, friends.

That said, it's really not as bad as you'd think. I have used a Diva Cup for years and after the first few times, you kind of get over it. It's no different than using a tampon, really.

You dump the contents into the toilet, wash or wipe out the cup, and reinsert. It takes less than a minute and you are spared the ordeal of a late-night tampon run where you invariably end up with the cutest cashier and you try and hide the tampons under a magazine and some Cheetos but he obviously has to scan them some time and now you've wasted seven dollars on useless camouflage purchases and are stuck with a copy of *Architecture Weekly* and your life is ruined—*ruined!*

Anyway!

If the idea of a menstrual cup is too extreme for you, or you can't even say "menstrual cup" without throwing up in your mouth a little, there are still a few options to reduce the amount of pollution generated by your lady time.

First of all, I just need to check that you aren't using plastic tampon applicators. You're not—right? Because you know that they're *plastic* and get used for all of five seconds and then languish in landfills for hundreds of thousands of years, and *do we need to talk about the cormorants again?* I don't even think we need to go into all this; you're on it, which is why you're using cardboard applicators, or even better, no applicators at all! I love you. Let's skip ahead.

For those of you who prefer pads, reusable cloth pads will be your new best friend. If you're crafty (I'm jealous), you can probably whip some up yourself in no time flat. They're typically made up of a cotton or fleece outer layer, with liners of absorbent cotton or hemp inside, and snaps or Velcro to attach securely around your underwear like an adhesive pad would.

If you're like me, however, and you've never used a sewing machine in your life, you can usually find cute cloth pads in your local health food store, sometimes at farmers markets, and definitely made by crafty types on Etsy.com. These work in the same way conventional pads do, but just get tossed in the washer to be reused instead of getting thrown out.

Cloth pads don't contain any of that weird and wonderful moisture-absorbing magic so you may have to change them more often than disposable pads, but the bonus is that they tend to be far less bulky, and they have zero packaging too.

I'd also like to take this opportunity to go on a tangential feminist rant, just because I can:

There's a strange element of shame involved in the marketing and advertising of feminine hygiene products, and it is somewhat ingrained in us to be disgusted or repulsed by the process of menstruation. Thus the never-ending production and purchase of these disposable products designed to keep us at arm's length from the process, so that we might never have to see, touch, or smell anything as intimate as our own bodies.

It's blood. We're women. Super-powerful, self-cleaning, beautiful, menstruating women, *damn it*. I don't want to my daughter to ever feel ashamed of her body by trying to keep her period a state secret lest somebody find out that—gasp!—she's undergoing a completely normal physiological process.

Furthermore, to deal with this completely normal physiological process we certainly don't need corporations selling us products that, due to their disposable nature, have an incredibly deleterious effect on our favorite woman of all, good ol' Mother Earth.

Let's respect her body by respecting our own. Ignore the commercials and the packaging and the plastic and that *ridiculous* blue liquid. Choose sustainable, choose to support crafty women, and choose to stop being grossed out or embarrassed by your period.

Period.

HAIR REMOVAL

Ugh. Say it with me now: UGGGH. This is the worst. I totally get why men grow beards.

Not everyone chooses to remove every strand of body hair that society deems unattractive, but, if you do, this section will cover all manner of hair removal for men and women, and we're going to dive in headfirst with the old standby: the razor.

Quick and efficient, albeit with short-lived results, the razor is many people's de-furring weapon of choice. I'm encouraged by its popularity, because it is actually fairly easy to put a green spin on this particular grooming ritual.

First, we have to ditch the daisy razors—no more plastic disposables.

Aside from the fact that they don't work very well even when brand-new, I find that after three or four uses it feels like you're hacking away at your stubble with a rusty butter knife. By the time they've seen three or four uses they end up getting tossed in the trash and dang, that's a whole lot of wasted plastic.

Marginally better, though still horrifically wasteful, are the razors where you replace only the head. You're trashing less, but still buying things just to throw out, and seriously, have you *seen* how expensive those replacement blades are? So pricey that they get locked up behind protective Plexiglas at the drug store. That's ridiculous! They're *razor*s, not diamonds.

The best option for tackling this waste is, in my humble opinion, to buy a double-edged razor. You know, the old-timey ones that take metal razorblades. That's right, instead of scraping a million-dollar aloe-infused six-bladed monstrosity over your tender cheeks each morning, use one blade instead that works really, really well.

If you want to go the extra mile, you can even avoid purchasing something new by sourcing a vintage razor at antique stores or sites like Etsy. Just make sure to boil or otherwise disinfect your secondhand beauty before use.

Replacement blades can be found at almost any drugstore or pharmacy and are ridiculously inexpensive (around three to four dollars for five blades).

And if you're kind of choked up about losing that hokey aloe-infused moisturizing strip, buy some actual aloe! It's sitting on the shelf two aisles over—unlocked.

For men, this option is not only eco-friendly, but also irresistibly appealing. I have no idea why, but there's something about walking into a guy's bathroom and seeing an old-timey razor kit—complete with shaving brush and mug soap—that sets him apart from the crowd. It's a kind of meticulousness that says, "I am one classy dude," without having to shell out for a cliché like a sports car or cashmere socks.

Ladies, we can use these razors too—just because they're not pink doesn't mean we can't play! They work incredibly well, and their larger width makes shaving your legs a quick five-minute affair, instead of having to futz about shaving one teensy strip at a time.

Shaving cream

Aerosol cans, plus chemically derived fragrances, plus weird foaming agents = no bueno. But don't worry; it's easy to get that smooth shave without.

To shave your face you can buy the aforementioned mug soap at most drugstores. It's called mug soap because it's a disc of soap that sits at the bottom of a mug, meant to be applied to the face with a shaving brush.

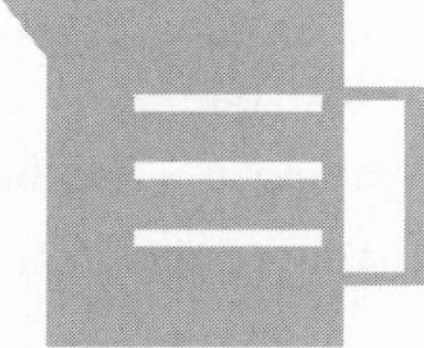

Alternately, often your local soap maker will offer a natural shaving soap that will be a bit gentler on both the environment and that sensitive just-shaved skin.

For larger areas like legs, chest, etc., or if you don't mind forgoing the suds, substitute coconut oil for your shaving cream. It makes for the smoothest shave ever at a fraction of the price, and far less waste too. Just be careful that you don't slip if you're using it in the bath or shower.

OK, now that we've got shaving covered, let's delve into other hair removal strategies.

Depilatory cream

I don't know what to say about this one. It's a chemical cream in a plastic bottle that literally burns the hair off of your body.

GUYS, IT *BURNS* THE HAIR OFF OF YOUR BODY! WITH CHEMICALS!

Seriously, this is some messed-up business. It's like something an evil Bond villain would dream up while dispassionately stroking a hairless cat! And honestly, I'm all about options and working with what you've got, but, try as I might, I really can't think of any eco-friendly options for depilatory devotees, aside from encouraging you to find another method to de-fuzz yourself.

Waxing

Waxing is great because it is quick and effective, and it offers the longest-lasting results of any do-it-yourself hair removal method. The downside is that most waxes contain resins, preservatives, and artificial colors and fragrances, and really, getting waxed is bad enough without worrying about the contents of the chemical stew being slathered all over your nether regions.

If for some reason you enjoy having hair ripped off of your most tender body parts but are searching for a less toxic way to do it—boy, do I have a solution for you!

You can avoid any nasties found in store-bought wax by sugaring instead. Sugaring is pretty much exactly what it sounds like—a simple paste made of sugar, water, and lemon juice boiled down until it's thick enough to use like you would hair-removal wax.

If you use cloth strips when sugaring, you'll find yourself with a natural, waste-free way to get yourself looking like one of those creepy hairless Chihuahuas in no time flat.

INGREDIENTS

2 cups sugar

¼ cup lemon juice

¼ cup water

Cloth wax strips

Wooden spatula

Candy thermometer

Mix all the ingredients together in a heavy saucepan over medium-high heat. Stir constantly until the candy thermometer reaches 250 degrees. (I've heard of people eyeballing the mixture and declaring it done when it develops the color of honey, but I have trouble getting the consistency right without the thermometer—cook it too long and it becomes too tough to spread, not long enough and it doesn't remove the hair properly.)

Also: PLEASE, for the love of Oprah, be careful when you're stirring, pouring, and handling the sugar paste. It's basically liquid hot magma, and not only could it potentially cause pretty severe burns, but it is sticky and would be a huge pain to get out of carpets or clothing. (For flat surfaces, utensils, etc., hot water will do the trick.)

Once it has reached 250 degrees, remove from heat and allow to cool a bit, then pour it into a canning jar and let it cool completely. (This isn't the time to bust out all those pickle jars—save those for your coffee. This stuff is 250 degrees, remember? You want to make sure you're using a jar that will be able to tolerate that heat, and canning jars fit the bill perfectly.)

You can either use the wax as soon as it's cool, or put it aside and pop it in the microwave the next time you want to use it (ten seconds should be plenty).

When the time comes, make sure it's not too hot, and then use a wooden spatula to spread a thin layer over the area you'd like to wax. Press a cloth strip firmly over the sugar paste, rub it several times to adhere the sugar to the strip, and then count to ten before ripping it off.

(Maybe count to fifteen, or one hundred, or if you're me, start moaning "Oh god, I can't do it. I can't do it! Help! Can someone else do it for me?" and wait for your sadistic husband to come to your rescue).

Repeat as necessary to remove all the hair from your person. With any luck you will emerge looking beautiful and smooth, and tasting a little sweeter too.

The cloth strips can be soaked in hot water to remove any excess paste and then laundered as normal.

CHAPTER 3
Lifestyle

BEING GREEN IS GOOD FOR THE WAISTLINE

Oh, guys, we are so ridiculous sometimes. I mean can we just take a moment to acknowledge our cumulative ridiculousness?

We spend millions of dollars on products that promise to make our lives easier so that we don't have to even scrub our own toilets anymore, and then, *then* we buy more useless gizmos—powders and shakes and ab-rollers (OH MY!)—to help us lose weight, weight that we have probably gained precisely because we have outsourced all the aforementioned toilet scrubbing, and are left, as a result, with increasingly tighter waistbands and tighter schedules to boot.

In our quest for an easier life it can sometimes seem like we've created three problems for every one we've tried to solve. Yes, harsh cleaners can eliminate the need for scrubbing, but they cause breathing problems, redden our hands, and result in mountains of plastic bottles in landfills. Cheap, widely available clothing has reduced the need for tailoring, but we now have closets stuffed to the brim with ill-fitting, poorly made clothing that gets stretched out after one wash and then just sits there taking up space.

Nowhere is this one-step-forward-two-steps-back thinking more evident than in the way many of us treat physical activity. It becomes one more chore added to our crammed to-do lists, right behind taking out the garbage and scooping dog poop. We are so pressed for time that taking care of ourselves is often the first thing to get bumped and, guys, that is some real BS right there.

You are important. Your health and well-being are important—far more important than garbage and dog poop, yes?

One of the most common complaints I hear about using natural cleaning recipes and taking steps toward a more eco-friendly lifestyle in general is that it requires too much work.

I'm not going to be a dick and pretend that it doesn't and then conveniently disappear when you emerge after a marathon cleaning session dripping in sweat and baking soda. Here it is: Yes, sometimes it *does* take a little more time and effort to use eco-friendly cleaning methods. There's no way around it.

BUT here is where that actually works to our benefit rather than our detriment: That time spent scrubbing out a tub, or hanging laundry, or even choosing to walk instead of driving ten blocks—this isn't wasted time. Rather than compartmentalizing your life into carefully delineated segments—"This is cleaning time. This is eating time. This is exercising time"—you can just *live.*

All these things that seem like such hard work are hard because you're expending energy and burning calories. These things are free, they don't require a gym membership or fancy equipment and they are an integral part of a whole life, rather than just one aspect of a fragmented one.

Choosing to clean with manual abrasives rather than chemical ones, choosing natural foods rather than packaged and processed, avoiding excess and overconsumption—these are the sort of "eco-friendly" habits that can also contribute to a smaller waistline and a healthier heart without compulsive dieting or beating yourself up at the treadmill.

Just live your life! More often than not you'll find that the choices that are healthiest for you will also be healthy for the environment.

QUICK TIP

Many municipalities now allow you to safely dispose of your end-of-life electronics at recycling centers. Call your municipality, or ask around to find an electronics recycling center in your area. (Alternately, if you're my husband, you could just greedily hoard every single video game console, clock radio, and tube television you have ever owned until your attic eventually begins to resemble a pawn shop from the '90s.)

So, you know, whatever. (P.S. Does anyone need a VCR?)

HOME, SWEET HOME

Do you know what the average home size was in 1950?

983 square feet.[6]

Nine-hundred-and-eighty-three square feet for an entire family. That's like the size of those fake IKEA apartments where they show you the joy of small-space living when you only own seven items of clothing, four forks, and two books.

Nine-hundred-and-eighty-three square feet. That seems absolutely incomprehensible to us now, even to me who has lived in sweet tiny houses for years.

Contrast that statistic to 2011, when the average family home ballooned up to 2,480 feet, almost triple the square footage. As astonishing as it may seem that in just sixty years we saw the size of our homes increase in size threefold, these numbers reveal something more than just our modern-day penchant for bigger floor plans. Not only are our homes three times the size, but the size of the families occupying these homes has shrunk considerably—from an average of 3.37 people in 1950, to just 2.6 today.

So our houses are bigger, our families smaller. With fewer people than ever occupying our homes, why exactly do we need all this extra space?

Well, the $22-*billion*-dollar-a-year home storage and organization industry may be able to provide us with an answer: We need that extra 1,527 square feet for all our *stuff*.

The availability of easily acquired consumer goods means that we have more possessions than ever before, and what we own is quickly beginning to own us.

The same study that gave us the statistics above also reported finding that almost a third of women's stress levels peaked during the times when they were dealing with their belongings.[7] This means that for many women the most *stressful* part of their day was not when they were working, not when refereeing World War III between bickering children, or even when they were stuck in rush-hour traffic, but simply when they were dealing with all their stuff.

This isn't exactly what we envisioned, is it?

I've racked my brains for a way to approach this without sounding like either a sanctimonious know-it-all or a holier-than-thou minimalist, but I don't know that there's any way around it: there's no way to tell people that they need to stop buying so much crap without sounding like kind of a jerk.

If someone said that to me I'd probably become incensed. "That turquoise ceramic Buddha figurine isn't *crap!* And neither are those tiny succulents that decorate my windowsill (fake, of course, because I kill any live plants within a week or two). And if you think these eight throw pillows are *junk*, you are out of your MIND!"

There would be some huffing and some puffing, perhaps I'd even storm off and slam the door, depending on how dramatic I felt that day. But then—and here's the rub—then I would sit there in my bedroom feeling like a petulant thirteen-year-old girl and I would think to myself, "Wow, jerk. You're *right.*"

Imagine your home with 25 percent—or if you like to live on the edge, 50—less *stuff.* Imagine having an empty shelf (or even *two*). Imagine having free space in your closet. Imagine having room to move and play and live, without stubbing your toe on that console table you found on sale. Imagine being able to actually park your car in your garage or find a muffin pan without getting buried under an avalanche of cookware.

I don't think I'm the only one who finds herself fantasizing about space, the sheer joy of an empty room and an uncluttered expanse of floor. But if you're anything like me, when you're imagining these things, you're not picturing this occurring in your own house. (Impossible! Your house is cramped and frustrating and entirely *too small!*) You're picturing a new house, a bigger house. A house that could offer you all the open space and bare shelves and room to grow that you'd ever need.

But let's continue this game of make believe for a second, beyond envisioning this big new house. Let's continue to the day after you move in, as you are padding around the polished hardwood floors in your socks, navigating towers of boxes with a mugful of steaming coffee in hand.

What do you do as you are walking around your new home? As you walk around, you begin to mentally decorate, of course. A rug here, a sectional there. Built-in bookshelves flanking the fireplace. Framed pictures and vases of flowers and, yes, perhaps even a turquoise ceramic Buddha figurine.

Cut to a few months down the road. Your bank account is emptier, and your house is once again crammed with belongings—no more bare shelves, no more empty closet space.

Our belongings expand to fill the space we provide for them.

That's the secret. That's how sane, full-grown adults can live in 428 square feet (like my mom does in her two-bedroom floating house), and why even a 2,500-square-foot home can feel like it's never big enough. It's never the *space* that's the problem. It's your *stuff.*

This is why so many of us fail at organization. Our intentions are good, and our hearts are in the right place. We watch the shows and read the articles, follow the steps and buy the color-coordinated bins and baskets. We tidy and arrange and file and breathe a huge sigh of relief when everything is all tickity-boo.

But a week later, when all has descended into chaos again—because really, who has the time to spend organizing and filing and putting way our belongings into all those baskets and bins eighteen times a day?—it's even more disheartening than before. Plus, on top of everything else, now we have to find a place for all these bins!

Let's stop kicking ourselves over this, OK? I give you full permission to foist at least part of the blame on the dysfunctional society that surrounds us. We are being sold two entirely disparate and incompatible ideals, and it's no wonder we are overwhelmed and frustrated.

On one hand we are surrounded by a relentlessly consumer-oriented culture that pervades every aspect and facet of our lives. Catalogs drop through the mail slot, sale alerts clog our emails, deal websites pop up on every browser, and it's almost impossible to go anywhere without coming face to face with millions of advertising dollars strategically spent to entice, coerce, and trick you into opening your wallet.

On the other hand we—and I'm looking especially at you, sistafriends—we are being sold a domestic goddess fantasy where our homes are always spotless, our laundry baskets empty, our garages relentlessly organized.

Unless you are willing to spend hours and hours and *hours* every week organizing and tidying, or you are ridiculously wealthy and can afford an almost infinite amount of space, these two ideals are completely incompatible.

You cannot have it all. Because then you have to store it somewhere.

All you need is less.

For the sake of the environment, your wallet, and yes, even your sanity: stop.

Stop shopping, stop buying, and stop organizing. Let's remember that dear ugly duckling from Chapter 1, and begin reducing. How you choose to do this is up to you. Some people leave their credit cards at home so that they have to think about a purchase overnight before committing to it. Others like to shop by wandering around the store and filling their carts with all the things they'd like to buy, and then abandon it before the checkout—enjoying the process of shopping without dealing with the results.

As for me, I conquered this particular habit entirely accidentally, by moving to a small town where shopping was heartbreakingly nonexistent, and then moving within this town to a series of three houses, each smaller than the last.

My shopping ceased almost altogether, especially for silly little home tchotchkes, and each time we moved we had to pare down our belongings more and more to fit the confines of our new space.

At first, it was difficult. I missed shopping. I missed decorating. I missed finding that perfect thing that I never even knew I needed until I saw it sitting prettily on a store shelf.

Over time it became easier, it got better, and I began to love it. On my increasingly rare shopping trips I grew accustomed to admiring things and then putting them back on the shelf. I grew used to always having an empty cardboard box at the bottom of my closet so that, when I pulled out something to wear in the morning and suddenly realized I loathed it, I could just throw it into the box to donate rather than hanging it back up.

I joined a buy-and-sell group on a social network site, which allowed me to sell little things as they outlived their purposes, rather than hoarding them until I had enough to host a full-blown garage sale.

In the beginning our tiny home set limits for me with its single closet, scaled down floor plan, and complete lack of a dining room. But by the time we moved I was beginning to set my own limits for how many possessions I would allow to possess me.

WHY *BEG, BARTER, BORROW* SHOULD BE THE NEW *EAT, PRAY, LOVE*

Late at night Adam and I walk our dog through silent neighborhoods. Together our footsteps echo on the cold concrete of sidewalks and crunch the crisp gravel of empty roads.

We like to walk slowly with big Gus, and peer in windows as we walk by, because we're creeps like that.

Almost every time we do this—our eyes lingering on the space between drawn curtains, taking in the activity and the blue glow of televisions—one of us remarks how strange it is that these houses exist. We marvel that the people inside of them exist, that their whole LIVES —complete with childhood memories and faded scars, allergies and failed relationships—their whole lives exist and we don't feature anywhere in them except maybe by chance, crossing the street in the background one sunny day downtown. Or waiting behind them in line at the grocery store, exhaling impatiently when the cashier's till breaks down.

It is somewhat impossible to wrap one's mind around, all these lives being lived. Each one of us has a mother and father, and in North America, a host of objects we call "mine." Each of us has shoes—at *least* one pair, if not ten. And couches, blenders, lawn mowers. We each own these things, tiny check marks in a list of essential possessions, so that walking through a neighborhood while the realization of this washes over you becomes a bizarre study in redundancy.

"This house has a lawn mower," we say as we pass it, Gus giving the lawn a cursory sniff.

"And this one," as we pass the next.

"And this one, and this one, and this one, and *this* one...." Our footsteps echo beneath our words as we catalogue these assets, these redundant possessions.

On and on and on. An infinite line of houses in an infinite number of neighborhoods, each with a lawn mower and not *just* a lawn mower, but a power washer, a food processor, fancy china, and somewhere in the back of a closet an elegant dress that's only been worn once.

I'd like to rewrite the book on this redundancy. I'd like the idea of *Beg, Barter, Borrow* to catch fire and become this year's *Eat, Pray, Love*. And yes, all right, a book about how you went next door and borrowed your neighbor's lawn mower is probably not going to be a bestseller any time soon, but that's OK. I'm fine with that, because instead of being on a navel-gazing mission to *find ourselves*, we're trying instead to find ways to reduce the need to shout "MINE!" and continually add to the clutter of objects that we use only occasionally.

There's no rule that says that you have to own everything. A lawn mower, a food processor, a car. Often, we own these things because we think they tell people something about who we are (someone with no cupboard space?). Or we like to have them for the one or two times a year when we need them, but for the remainder of the time they just sit there unused and gathering dust.

Communal property tends to be avoided like the plague these days, and I'm not sure why. Perhaps we're afraid of creating that connection, having to talk to someone and knock on their door, ask for help, and become indebted.

Perhaps we're afraid of getting burned, afraid of lending something only to have it mistreated, or ruined. (I definitely understand this one as the eldest of five girls and the owner of many items of clothing worn once and then destroyed by a sneaky sister.)

But perhaps, *perhaps* the practice has grown so out of use that joint ownership or communal property or *sharing* just doesn't occur to us anymore.

The availability of credit cards and proliferation of easily acquired consumer goods means that we very rarely have to do without, and we usually find ourselves asking, "Why borrow something when I can own it?" because owning is always assumed to be the best option.

By owning each and every single thing that we could ever need at any point in the conceivable future, we lose out on precisely those connections we would form by doing without. We don't get to know our neighbors; we don't build the web of small kindnesses that is formed by lending and borrowing, or by exchanging one service for another.

If two households pooled their resources they could potentially cut their possessions, their expenses, and the space needed to store those possessions in half. We teach our children to share, we constantly espouse the values of cooperation and collaboration and helping others, so why not put our money where our mouths are?

This could work with a neighbor or a friend or even a family member who lives close by. And we don't have to get all crazy and litigious about it either.

When I first began writing this chapter I thought of suggesting that you draw up a contract or make an agreement, something with rules and guidelines and clauses and consequences. I thought of creating safeguards to prevent anyone from getting burned. But honestly, I think that is making things far more complicated than it needs to be—guys, just use your best judgment.

Try approaching a friend or neighbor and offering them the use of something of yours. Be generous, be open. And then, when you need something, feel OK about asking to borrow it. The worst they can say is no. If you know them well enough or if you feel comfortable, you could even work out an exchange of services (e.g., you can borrow her lawn mower if you do her lawn too).

Make sure you lend to those who take care of their things, make sure you treat what you borrow the way you would treat your own. Say please, say thank you, be kind and smile. Basic stuff, really.

Perhaps, just perhaps, Ms. Jones owns a lawn mower and Mr. Smith owns a carpet cleaner. They work out an agreement where each is used as needed and returned when not. Together their lawns are manicured and their carpets spotless, and maybe in this sweet little exchange of lawn maintenance tools and floor cleaning devices, maybe they begin to fall in love.

Hands touch while opening a garage door; eyes meet over a half-empty container of rug shampoo. Over time their excuses for mowing their lawns and cleaning their carpets become more and more outlandish. They begin to share more than just their possessions; they begin to share their *hearts.*

True love found through a mutual distaste of overconsumption. Now *that's* a book I would read.

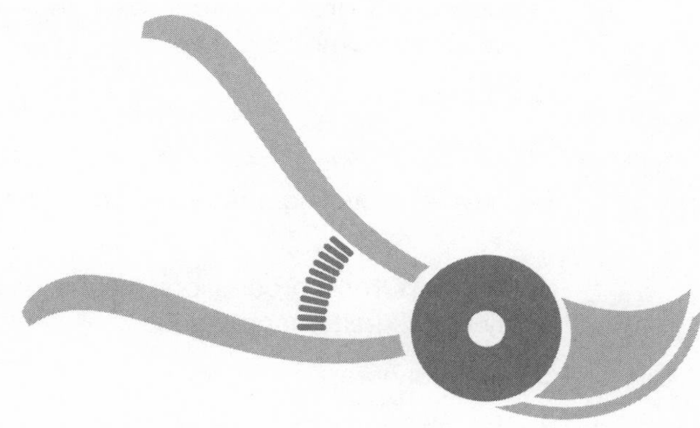

QUICK TIP

Some ideas for things that are great to beg, barter, and borrow

- A large set of inexpensive dishes and cutlery used for parties and outdoor soirées
- Yard maintenance equipment (lawn tractors, chainsaws, pressure washers, snow blowers, etc.)
- Tools
- Space in your greenhouse in exchange for a cut of any vegetables grown
- Child care
- Dog walking
- Terracycle recycling brigades (more info on pages 45–46)
- Dehydrators, food processors, mixers, or other rarely used kitchen appliances
- Carpet cleaners
- Books, children's toys, board games, movies, video games, etc.
- Air mattresses/blow-up guest beds

HOW TO REMEMBER YOUR REUSABLE BAGS

Yeah, I know you know.

We ALL know. We know we're not supposed to be using plastic bags, we've all jumped on the bandwagon and embraced the concept and bought cloth bags and then we've all forgotten said bags, again and again and again and again, because they seem to be *everywhere* until you actually need them.

It's gotten to the point where supermarket checkouts have become confessionals of sorts. How many times have you inched your way toward the cashier as if she were a makeshift priest, your face flushed and your heart pounding?

How many times have you watched her snap her gum and stare at you dispassionately as you laid your sins at her feet and confessed in an embarrassed whisper, "Oh gosh, I'm *so* sorry. I forgot my bags *again*."

I have no doubt that our hearts are in the right place, but alas, many of us have the memory span of a goldfish. That's OK, though, because instead of berating you for forgetting your cloth bags, I'm going to try to help you find ways to remember them.

First, we're going to continue beating this metaphor to death. Good Catholics out there, please tell me, what happens after you have made your confession?

Adam, a Catholic by birth, is staring at me blankly, but the rest of you are correct! Penance! (Penance is a fancy word for punishment). That's right, you have to pay the price for the unforgivable sin of forgetting your cloth bags, but you can put away your rosary and stop mumbling Hail Marys. That's really not helping anything.

Your penance, my friend, is that, if you don't have bags, *you don't have bags.*

You read that right.

If you forget your bags, you have to turn down the plastic stand-ins, and take your purchases without.

It's going to suck. *A lot.* Especially if you have $200 worth of groceries that you now have to load into your car and then unload into your kitchen one by goddamn one. Now is probably a good time to take a shot of whisky, or try out those fancy new swear words you heard your nephew using, and I give you full permission to channel your frustration into drawing a mustache on my author photograph too, but whatever you do, you whisky-swilling, trucker-mouthed blasphemer, *do not get plastic bags.*

Trust me when I say that you have to stick to this.

There's a perfectly reasonable explanation for this eco-masochism, and it's not just because I enjoy watching people juggle kumquats and arugula. The reason is that this experience will be so horrific, and so infuriating, and so utterly *humiliating* as you load your purchases one by one into the grocery cart with the entire line-up behind you watching in bemused confusion, that it will be forever burned into your psyche.

The next time you step out of your car on the way to go grocery shopping, memories of making seventeen trips to and from your front door with armfuls of kale and pork chops will wash over you like a wave. Your hands will tremble and your face will flush, and mark my words: *you will remember your cloth bags.*

You're welcome.

QUICK TIP

Some other helpful ways to reduce plastic bag use that don't involve self-flagellating displays of penitence:

Keep a compact reusable bag in your purse for those spur-of-the-moment purchases

Refuse a plastic bag for five items or less

Fit purchases from different stores into the same bag wherever possible. There's no reason to have eight shopping bags with only one item in each. (Bonus: It looks like you only went to one store. Such restraint!)

Put your cloth bags back in your car as soon as you're done unloading groceries. There's less chance of forgetting them at home that way (and you'll be one step closer to using them!).

Keep them on the front seat, rather than in the trunk. If you see them, you'll be far less likely to forget them.

ADDICTIONS

This may seem like a strange topic to discuss in a book about eco-friendly tips and tricks, but addictions and environmentalism are more closely connected than you might think, and I'm not even talking about my strange addiction to clean floors, or how I get all tingly when I get a new essential oil. (Adam would like me to point out that these are too lame to qualify as true addictions.)

No, the addictions I'm talking about can be boiled down to one word: wanting. Or two words: instant gratification.

We have become incredibly uncomfortable with wanting—not wanting and getting (we are, I think, a little *too* comfortable with that process), but just *wanting* in and of itself. Desiring something without being able to attain it. It's rarely enough to feel the irresistible pull of lust and attraction to an object, to imagine yourself possessing it, to imagine who you would be if you had it.

No, the desire must be satiated and the wanting must be cured by *getting*, even though we all know deep down (and studies agree) that much of the fun is in the wanting itself.

This state of impatience, of permanently acquiring without ever pausing to savor the acquisition itself, contributes to all manner of modern-day evils: infidelity, debt, obesity, crime, depression, Facebook. They're all addictions of some sort, and they're all spurred by wanting without being able to stop getting.

I wonder if we can be content with just wanting. And I wonder what it would take for us to realize that, every time one desire is fulfilled, another crops up in its place.

This isn't all metaphysical speculation either. The implications of this airy theoretical discussion have very real results, namely that if we don't stop mindlessly scratching the itch of want-fulfilling, our lives become like an infuriating game of whac-a-mole, where the stakes are far higher than a stuffed toy or a sweaty handful of tickets. At stake is that ever-elusive state of feeling contented.

At stake is feeling that you have *enough*.

Think about it: when was the last time you thought to yourself, "This is good enough"?

It feels lazy, somehow, doesn't it? Isn't that *settling?* Shouldn't we be constantly striving for better, more, higher, faster, bigger? Why would we ever say "*Enough*"?

Consuming becomes an addiction far before it gets to the stage where you would be eligible to appear on the next season of *Hoarders*. Inadequacy is a drug being pushed by every single commercial and advertisement and billboard that tells you your teeth aren't white enough, your clothing isn't clean enough, and your children will love you more if you buy them multi-colored fruit snacks.

Everything around us, from advertising to the way products are being made in an increasingly disposable fashion, contributes to this state of perpetual wanting, and it is incredibly unhealthy.

By pointing this out, I don't mean to imply that I am above this in any way. I go shopping, I'm obsessed with Pinterest, I too find myself stuck here at this game of whac-a-mole, rubber mallet in hand, alternating wildly between railing at the system and wanting desperately to avail myself of its trappings.

But I think that simply being aware of this state goes a long way toward combating it. And here is where it ties in with the environmental movement: The addiction to this disposable life is no different than an addiction to food, or smoking, or any other unhealthy pattern of behavior. At its core lies a deep-seated feeling of inadequacy, and this feeling is so desperately uncomfortable that we seek to quash it any way we can. With another mouthful of cake or one more drink, a new pair of shoes or an amazing vacuum cleaner that promises to change our lives.

More and more, our identities are determined not by the way we choose to live our lives, but by the products we buy. When those products become old and outdated, replaced by newer, shinier models, where does that leave us?

Lately these identities are being carefully edited to include "green" living. Choosing an eco-friendly life has become suddenly trendy and fashionable and, more than that, something you are judged on. You're identified as being "green" by the items you consume—the reusable shopping bags with witty sayings on them, all those cute travel mugs (bought and lost, and bought again).

For many people, being eco-friendly has become just another source of inadequacy, one more thing to feel guilty for not doing, and that's really not what it should be about. Women in particular are prone to this. We are so hard on ourselves, we heap blame and judgment upon our shoulders and lob it at others, we let this guilt fester until we feel so bad that we throw money at the problem, hoping it will simply go away. But the guilt fuels feelings of inadequacy, and inadequacy fuels consumption, and consumptions fuels guilt, and we get stuck in this cycle, and—yes, friends—it *is* an addiction.

Are you crying? Are we fighting? Do you need a drink?

I'm sorry to get all heavy on you, and I promise that my little pop-psychology lesson is almost over. And if you skipped that whole long diatribe (I don't blame you), just take away these few words: Living an eco-friendly lifestyle is more than buying eco-friendly stuff; it's breaking the addiction to feeling that you need all that *stuff* in the first place.

You become a good person not because of what you buy, but because of what you *do*.

If I learned anything from working with at-risk teens fighting substance abuse problems, it is that the key to successful recovery lies in identifying and treating the root cause of an addiction, rather than simply addressing its outward symptoms.

So, if you're sitting there feeling guilty because you're not a card-carrying member of the eco-elite and you are overwhelmed, stressed, and confused about where to start, start by stopping.

Then just take it one day at a time.

MAKE IT

Clothesline

Drying our clothes outside was something I put off for quite a while. To be honest, it seemed like a lot of work. Rather than just throwing laundry from the washer to the dryer, I would have to haul a heap of damp clothing outside, individually clip each item to the clothesline, and then remember to come back later to take everything in again.

In the meantime anything could happen—rain, wind, or even nosey neighbors laughing at my dainties. Despite my misgivings, however, when we rented

a small house with a gorgeous backyard, I knew I had to give it a try. I'm not very handy, so I opted to purchase an inexpensive clothesline kit from my local hardware store for under forty dollars, but it would be simple to rig one up yourself if you had a little know-how. To get really basic you'd need little more than a rope strung between two trees, but it might be more work in the long run as you'd be missing the pulleys and would have to move along the line, clipping as you went.

Alternately, there are stand-alone clothing racks that require no installation at all, making them a great option for renters as well as those with small (or nonexistent) backyards. I have one that I use indoors during the winter months and it works like a hot damn, but if you go this route make sure you don't cheap out and buy a flimsy one or you'll be enraged every time you use it. If you're really stuck, I had a friend who used to simply drape her stuff over a garden hedge. Hey, whatever works—right?

Anyway, on the first sunny day after I had installed our clothesline (and by "I," I mean "Adam, under great duress"), I grudgingly hauled a basket of wet laundry into the backyard and began hanging our clothes.

I was approaching this whole thing as a Great Sacrifice. There was Madeleine, nobly doing What Was Right at great personal inconvenience, spurning the convenience of indoor laundry facilities For The Greater Good. I was the perfect martyr!

But guys, I found it so meditative, it was insane. Pick up a shirt, pin, pin, slide the line over. Pick up a tea towel, pin, pin, slide the line over. Item after item, bamboo clothespin after bamboo clothespin. I continued this little repetition until my laundry basket was empty, then I stood back to survey my work.

I had a full line of clean clothing gently flapping in the breeze. My face was warm from the sun, my arms felt a pleasant sort of ache. It was so...*wholesome.*

All in all, it had taken only about ten minutes longer than hurriedly throwing everything into the dryer and pressing “Start,” and I’d been able to get outside and enjoy some sun and fresh air too.

I was hooked. Laundry, usually one of my most hated chores, suddenly became enjoyable. During the winter our laundry hampers sit stagnant and brimming until I finally run out of clean underwear, but during the warmer months the first thing I think of when I wake up to a sunny day is how much laundry I can get done.

(I am fully aware of how lame that sounds. But I’m too busy admiring my gently flapping clothes and feeling wholesome to care.)

I’m now a total convert and can’t wait for spring to arrive each year so I can get out of the laundry room and into our backyard. I’ve also found that the sun is an incredible whitener, especially for organic stains like sweat or dirty diapers, and clothing dries incredibly quickly—often in under thirty minutes on a hot or windy day.

Some people don’t like how clothing and towels get that slightly stiff, crunchy feeling from being line-dried. I love crisp sheets and look at crunchy towels as a means to a little extra exfoliation, but if the feeling bothers you, just pop them in the dryer for five minutes or so after they're dry, and you'll still come out ahead.

By using your dryer less you're not only saving a ton on energy bills—because the dryer is one of your household's most inefficient appliances—you're also prolonging the life of your wardrobe. Repeated tumble drying can cause clothing fibers to break down faster (think about the amount of stuff that ends up in your dryer's lint trap), and causes more wear and tear on clothing over time.

QUICK TIP

Some cities and homeowner's associations have placed ridiculous bans on backyard clotheslines, and this infuriates me so much that I could rant for days on end, but instead I will simply say that if this is the case in your neighborhood, I encourage you to channel your rage into a politely worded letter to your local government official or association president to protest this needless bureaucracy. Feel free to include bucolic pictures of sheets and baby clothes flapping in the sunshine for added effect.

Rain barrel

My mom has long lamented the fact that we don't have some sort of gray-water system in place in North America, and, when you think about it, she's totally right. Why are we flushing our toilets with drinking water? I mean it's great to have the loo as a backup source of hydration in the event of a zombie apocalypse or something, but it would be even greater if gray-water runoff from the sink or shower could be somehow rerouted to the toilet.

Clearly I have neither the intelligence nor the attention span to take on a project of this complexity, although I would happily claim some of the credit if it ever got invented, but I do have a suggestion for making use of waste water around your home that's a little simpler to adopt.

Finding a way to catch and store rainwater for use at a later date, for example, instead of just letting it hit the ground or run off into the gutters.

According to the EPA, 30 percent of domestic water use in peak summer months goes to maintaining lawns and gardens[8]—30 percent! That's a whole lot of our pristine, clean, filtered, and treated drinking water that's being poured out onto patches of grass and marigolds. I love flowers as much as the next gal, but given the imminent water shortage, we must find a better way.

A rain barrel is an easy and effective way of collecting and storing rainwater for later use. It eases the load on both your municipal water system and your water bill, as well as giving a treat to your plants, indoors and out: nothing is better for growing green than rainwater. I even have a friend who swears that nothing softens your hair like rinsing with rainwater (hippie high five!).

As with the clothesline, there are rain barrel kits readily available for purchase at most hardware stores or at specialty stores online (and many offer free shipping). A typical rain barrel will run you anywhere from $100 to $200, and typically includes a large vessel to hold the water as well as a screen on top to keep out insects and other debris. Some come with pieces to attach directly to your gutter's downspout to catch rainwater runoff from your roof; others are just open at the top to catch rainfall. If you can spring for it, a rain barrel with a hose attachment is incredibly convenient when it comes to using your catchings.

They say that when it rains it pours, and by using a rain barrel you are saving water from those "pouring" days to use on the scorching, earth-parching, hot hot HOT days when you run your hose dry trying to keep things alive. It's a great way to hack one of nature's natural processes, and you can save up to 1,300 gallons of water during the summer months.[9]

A few tips for the use and installation of these handy contraptions come from my dear brother Liam, who happily installed one last summer. All went well until this spring, two days before he listed his home for sale. After heading down to his basement to retrieve something, he found to his horror that a river ran through it.

His basement, I mean.

Turns out they'd had a record snowfall that winter (and when you break snowfall records in a Canadian city, we are talking about a LOT of snow), which was followed by a quick melt, and these two factors resulted in their rain barrel overflowing many, many, many times over and flooding their foundation.

Despite this initial hiccup—this costly, painful, fishing-in-your-basement-hiccup—he remains enthusiastic about his rain barrel and has not given up using it. He asked me to pass along these tips so that you don't accidentally end up with an unwanted water-feature:

- Install the rain barrel at least six feet from your house. Locating it near the area you'll be watering the most makes for convenient use later.
- Ensure that your rain barrel has an overflow at least as large as your inflow—for example, if you have rigged it so that water is collected directly from your eaves' trough downspout, your overflow valve should be as large as your downspout as well. This will allow your barrel to get rid of excess water as fast as it collects it, which might be necessary if you live in a city with crazy, unpredictable weather like my brother does.
- If you are using the rain barrel to water your garden, consider using a soaker hose. You can attach the hose to the rain barrel and then run it through your garden so that it covers the area you'd like. Then whenever your kale's looking a little thirsty, you don't have to stand there holding the hose like a chump, you just open the hose valve, walk away and let gravity do its work. (Lazy environmentalists for the win!)

QUICK TIP

Air fresheners are the worst. Never, ever use them. The bad ones disguise odors with over-the-top fragrances, the worst ones use strange chemical compounds to block the scent receptors in your nose. Better options include a) cleaning, removing, yelling at, or otherwise dealing with the stink at its malodorous source and then, b) making a natural air freshener by simmering a pot of water with a bit of lemon, ginger, cinnamon, cloves, vanilla, orange peels, or essential oils. Just make sure you don't leave the pot unattended.

CHAPTER 4

Food and Drink

EATING SIMPLY

No one who knows me in the slightest would ever call me a "foodie." Or a "good cook." Or even "able to competently create edible food on a consistent basis."

I have been known to refer to myself as the Amelia Bedelia of the kitchen because my mishaps are many and varied—exacerbated by the fact that I've been a vegetarian for my entire adult life but often try to cook meat dishes for Adam (because I am a GOOD WIFE).

My many meal misadventures include the time I literally could not tell a chicken's ass from its elbow and ended up cooking it upside down (a recipe now referred to as "Madeleine's Famous Upside Down Chicken" because it happily resulted in incredibly juicy chicken breasts), and the time I didn't realize that my husband had bought smoked salmon fillets, and I proceeded to cook them as though they were raw. I started to clue in when the recipe said the cooked fillets would "fluff lightly with a fork" and instead my fork got stuck and stood straight up.

In short, approximately three out of four culinary adventures end with me reminding Adam that it's the thought that counts. (Right?)

Now that I've offered up my own ineptitude for your enjoyment, it goes without saying that I won't be giving any cooking tips here. But, regardless of whether you are a gourmet chef or an amateur like me, whether you are trying to lose weight or gain weight or just eat more healthily, the way you grocery shop can have a huge impact on your health, your budget, and your carbon footprint. And shopping? Shopping is something I can *definitely* help you with.

Michael Pollan wrote a fantastic book called *In Defense of Food: An Eater's Manifesto*. In it he offered three simple tips for healthy eating, but the one that stuck with me the most was the ridiculously simple edict "Eat food."

What he meant by this was to eat *real* food, rather than the food-like substances that crowd much of the supermarket shelves. He suggested that if your great-grandmother wouldn't have recognized it, it should be off the menu.

This guideline is universally helpful in simplifying eating habits regardless of what particular *style* of eating you subscribe to—vegan, vegetarian, paleo, chocolate-covered, and so on.

Buying fresh ingredients; avoiding as much processed, packaged, and pre-made food as you can; and choosing to shop in local farmers markets and food co-ops whenever possible means you can make positive choices about not only *what* you're eating, but how it was grown or raised, the way it is packaged, and who is benefiting from the money you spend.

But I'll readily admit what most "eat-healthy!" advocates won't: sometimes, eating healthfully sucks. Seriously, let's be honest, it just does. Sometimes you want a brownie. Sometimes you want fast food. And sometimes the only thing stopping me from buying a gigantic bag of nachos and a jar of fluorescent orange *salsa con queso* is the shame of being seen by someone I know while I'm doing it.

That being said, *most* of the time I choose not to buy that not-found-in-nature snack because I simply don't feel good after I eat it. There's a five-second window of pure bliss, an itch scratched, a craving satiated, and then I feel like garbage.

It's a completely predictable sequence of events: There's the *queso* overdose coma, the shame, and then the half-empty jar mocking me from the countertop. All three mix together in a disgusting slurry of guilt and recrimination, and I usually end up feeling gross and vowing "Never again!"

Over time, as I have grown and matured and become an adult, I have realized that nothing about junk food actually feeds me—mind, body, or soul. So, for me at least, eating simply isn't about making rules, or setting limits, or depriving myself, but about making that connection between cause and effect. Realizing that those little "treats" make me feel worse, not better.

So I don't do it.

(Most of the time. I swear.)

In my world, eating simply also means trying to buck the current trend of throwing out almost 40 percent of the food that we purchase at grocery stores. (Seriously, that's a real statistic.)[10] I try to aim for a few smaller grocery shops throughout the week, rather than a big one where food is more likely to spoil as Sunday approaches.

Keeping it simple in terms of what you eat and where you shop, and making sure to finish what's in your fridge before you buy more, can do a lot to reduce unnecessary food waste.

REDUCING WASTE IN THE GROCERY STORE

If you're trying to decrease the amount of garbage produced by your household, you can make a big dent by choosing to not bring it into your home in the first place.

An awesome place to start is in the supermarket aisles. Here are some simple ways I've found to cheat the system. (By "cheat the system" I mean "cut down on garbage." But cheat the system sounds cool and vaguely hackerish, so use that):

Don't use produce bags. Every person in the grocery store has already fondled each and every fruit and vegetable on display, so don't kid yourself that individually bagging that head of lettuce or bell pepper is going to offer some magical shroud of cleanliness. Skip the bags and take them as is, I mean you're washing your veggies anyway, right?

Choose reusable bags for smaller produce, or bulk

items. Don't use the preceding tip for things like Brussels sprouts or pistachios. You will look crazy and your checkout person will hate you. Instead, you can use reusable bags made of cloth or mesh, fine enough to contain most small produce and bulk items with the exception of flour and spices. These bags can be purchased from some grocery stores and most health food stores.

Buy spices in bulk. If you've already got spice jars, buy spices in bulk to refill the jars rather than buying a new jar each time.

Rinse and reuse bags. When you do have to use plastic bags (e.g., for spices, as above), rinse out the bags and keep them with your reusable shopping bags so that you can use them again next time.

Avoid excess packaging. Choose items with little to no packaging whenever possible, and pass on individually wrapped items as well as those 100-calorie packs of chips or chocolate. Not only do they generate a ridiculous amount of waste, but they tend to be double or triple the price of the regular size. Plus, I have no doubt that you can calculate a 100-calorie serving on your own, if you so desire.

Shop the U. You can cut in half the amount of garbage, unhealthy food, *and* wasted money if you stick to shopping only the outer aisles of a grocery store—the meat, dairy, and fresh produce sections. And let's be honest here: there's nothing quite like the smug delight of going through the

> checkout with a shopping cart loaded to the top with only healthy items. (I mean, not that this should be your prime motivation, but oh, doesn't getting your smug on feel delicious sometimes?)

It can also help if you can learn how to make easy things like salsas, salad dressings, and common dips like tzatziki or hummus. This goes a long way toward reducing the amount of processed food you eat, as well as the amount of packaging you are buying and disposing of.

The Internet is incredibly helpful in learning to do this sort of thing. Right at your fingertips lie a million different recipes with step-by-step directions easy enough that even Amelia Bedelia herself could follow them. An added bonus is that no one has to know that you had never made homemade salsa in your life until you were twenty-seven years old.

(For example.)

QUICK TIP

Banana peels aren't just for slapstick hijinks anymore. They make great polish for leather shoes too. Just rub the inside of a peel evenly over your kicks, then gently buff to a shine with a soft cloth. You'll go bananas over how brand-new they look! (Sorry)

TAKING ON TAKEOUT

Adam and I were strolling around Vancouver one fine sunny day when we nipped into a chain coffee shop for a quick pick-me-up. As we stood in line to order our drinks, we looked around and suddenly noticed that every single person—even those who looked to be camped out for weeks buried under laptops and coffee-stained sheaves of paper—every single person had a disposable coffee cup.

It was astounding. Everywhere we looked, another cup! Littering tables and clutched in hands, and lo! Two large garbage cans flanking the door, filled to the brim with—you guessed it—coffee cups.

It was one of the strangest things I have ever seen, and the strangeness was compounded by the fact that we had probably seen this very same sight, and no doubt been a part of it hundreds of times before. Yet this time, *this time,* we were looking at our surroundings with new eyes.

I couldn't stop staring at those garbage cans, overflowing with cups that had been discarded after being used for no more than half an hour. *Never even leaving the coffee shop!* It made no sense, I felt like we were living in Bizarro World.

When it was our turn to order, I asked the barista if it was possible to get our drinks in real glasses. She looked momentarily surprised and then fumbled around behind the counter until she produced two large glasses, and, after happily paying for our ridiculous drinks, we were in business.

I was happy because I didn't have to throw out a coffee cup after using it for five minutes, Adam was happy because he thinks he got more Frappuccino for his fiver as the glasses were bigger, and I will venture a guess that even ol'

Mother Nature was a little bit happy, because we saved some trash from cluttering up the landfill.

This is one of those tiny changes that has the potential to make a huge difference on the landscape of our world with just a tiny bit of initiative on our part.

You see, most big coffee shops have actual mugs that they can use to serve your steamy latte in. Yes, real mugs! Made of ceramic, with that delicious hefty weight to them, and no plastic lid with a too-small hole for hot liquid to leap up and burn your lips through either. They're right there hiding behind the counter somewhere, and you'd probably never know they were there unless you asked.

That's because most of the time, unless you specifically state that you'd like your order in a "to-stay" cup, you'll get a disposable one. It's quicker and easier for the baristas, with the added bonus of zero cleanup. But of course all those disposable cups add up, and it's one level of crazy to use one if you're taking your coffee to go, but using them while you are actually *sitting there in the coffee shop*? No. I can't believe.

Please indulge me and be the person asking for a to-stay cup. You will look way classy, you won't have to fumble with a finicky plastic lid, and if you are anything like Adam it will make your day to think that you're getting a bit more bang for your buck.

Now, what if you are super-important and über busy and don't have time to just lounge around in coffee shops all day drinking out of mugs like the cast of *Friends?*

One solution that has become quite popular in recent years is to employ a reusable travel mug, but I find that the popularity of these mugs has caused them to proliferate to the point where they have become just one more useless item in and of themselves. Rather than reducing waste, they have *become* the waste.

We buy them, or we receive them as promos for a new gym or a radio station, or as prizes in contests, or as part of your swag bag at that work conference. We use them for a while before they break, or we lose the lid, or the plastic gets a funny taste and then the mug is banished to the back cupboard with three odd Tupperware lids and that ugly bowl your sister gave you that you only bring out whenever she comes to visit.

Travel mugs mean well, but in the process of trying to reduce waste, they're actually just creating more.

A solution that has worked out really well for me is to use jars in their place. It's a bit strange and I have definitely gotten the side-eye from more than one barista, but if you think about it, it makes total sense.

First of all, we all have jars, whether they're proper trendy mason jars or old pasta jars headed for the recycling bin. They're free, readily available, and almost all of them have lids that seal completely. This means that when you use jars you can literally toss your morning coffee in your purse—no more juggling files and purse and car keys, spilling all over yourself, and dappling your front with the drips my mom calls "seniors' buttons." Plus when you (inevitably) leave your coffee on top of your car or under the subway seat, it's not a huge deal because that olive jar was headed for the recycling bin anyway and you managed to get a few more uses out of it.

Since I started doing this it has caught on with quite a few of my friends, which is a very good thing for me because the more people that show up at Starbucks with pickle jars, the less crazy I look.

The final culprit in the waste-world of food and beverage takeout is the garbage created by takeout food—the containers, paper and Styrofoam plates, paper napkins, and plastic utensils.

Obviously the main way to combat this is to reduce or eliminate eating takeout completely, but for hapless chefs like me takeout food is sometimes a necessary evil. Even if you only order in or dine at mall food courts once or twice a year, the following tips can still reduce waste.

Firstly, carry your own utensils. This may be an easier tip for women to adopt, because our purses are already crammed with wallets, hand cream, lip gloss, pens, baby toys, and planners—I mean, in the face of all that noise, what's a few utensils thrown into the mix?

I use a sweet bamboo set that my sister-in-law got me one year for Christmas, but any old fork-knife-spoon set will do. Any time I am out somewhere that provides plastic cutlery, I just use my own instead. It's an easy way to avoid generating waste, and especially convenient if you want to pick up food from a grocery store to eat on the run.

The second way to reduce one-time-use items is to ask if you can bring your own containers when picking up takeout food. I sometimes get a bit of a baffled pause after I ask, but I've always been pleasantly surprised with how accommodating and pleasant restaurants are when faced with this request.

After you've done it a few times, no one will even blink an eye, and they might even start offering this option to other customers too. It never hurts to ask!

If you're getting your food delivered, ask what kind of containers they use. Try to order from restaurants that use cardboard or recyclable materials, rather than Styrofoam. If you do find yourself switching allegiances from one restaurant to another, you could even politely let them know why. Many restaurant owners find it hard to justify the increased cost of eco-friendly takeout containers, but if they know that it is costing them the business of hungry hippies like you, it could help sway their decision.

The reason you're trying to avoid takeout containers is because they're typically made of Styrofoam, which cannot be recycled and does not break down in landfills. Even the cardboard ones carry a big footprint for something that will be used only for five or ten minutes. Using your own containers is a simple way to reduce or eliminate waste from convenience food, and to reconcile your love of chow mien with your love of the planet.

Finally, consider picking up a set of inexpensive secondhand dishes from your local thrift store to use at kids parties, barbecues, and other situations when you would usually use paper or plastic dishes and utensils.

By having a "cheap" set, you won't be worried about broken plates or lost forks, you won't have an overflowing garbage at the end of the day, and, best of all, your guests can feel free to load on the salad fixins without fearing that a flimsy plastic plate will tip the whole thing into their laps.

QUICK TIP

Jars can get pretty hot with a steaming mocha inside, so I like to get cutesy and use a little crocheted sleeve. If you're not into grandma crafts like I am, you can also use the cuff off a sweater you don't wear anymore. The stretchy fabric will hug the jar and prevent your hands from getting scalded. A cute sock that's lost its mate would work well too.

MAKE IT

OK, I lied a little bit when I said there wouldn't be recipes. In my defense, these are so simple that a monkey could do them, and they require zero cooking, so they aren't really recipes so much as they are…directions. Directions for making food.

Shut up.

These four items are some of the only things that I can confidently make without a recipe, and they turn out great every time! (*Almost* every time!)

By making these myself from raw ingredients, I can avoid having to buy them in plastic containers, where they are full of mystery ingredients and preservatives too.

Punch-yourself-in-the-face salsa

So named because when I first made this, I couldn't believe how simple it was. I truly could not comprehend that I had spent twenty-seven years eating what was essentially chunky tomato paste from a plastic jug, when I could have been feasting on this magnificence.

In short, I felt like punching myself in the face for those lost salsa years, and also just because I couldn't deal with the sheer amazingness of it all.

INGREDIENTS

4–5 ripe tomatoes, diced. (Extra points if they are in season or from a farmers market or even your very own garden!)

2 jalapenos, seeded and finely chopped

Juice of 1 lime

1 teaspoon brown sugar

1 bunch cilantro, finely chopped

1 red onion, finely chopped

After you are done feeling like a real chef with all that slicing and dicing, combine all the ingredients in a large bowl and mix well. Let sit for about 15 minutes (if you can stand it), and then let the feast begin.

You can skip the tortilla chips altogether and just eat this with a spoon. It's that good. Seriously, I'm never buying salsa again.

Delicious tzatziki

Not face-punch worthy, but only because I need both hands to restrain myself from face-planting into this creamy wonder.

YOU NEED:

Cheesecloth or a clean tea towel

Cheese grater

3 cups thick plain Greek yogurt

1 cucumber

1 bunch fresh dill, stemmed and chopped

2 garlic cloves, crushed

Salt to taste

Wash the cucumber and grate it onto the cheesecloth or tea towel using the coarsest side of your cheese grater. Wrap it into the middle of the cheesecloth and gather the sides to squeeze all the juice out. You can either save this in a glass for a refreshing drink, discard it, or even use it as a soothing facial toner.

Combine the yogurt, grated and drained cucumber, dill, and garlic in a sealable container (the yogurt container works well for this). Mix well and then let sit for 1–2 hours to let the flavors emerge. Bliss.

Zero-electricity, cold brewed, basically-the-solution-to-global-warming coffee

We don't own a coffee maker. This is half because we're cheap, half because we don't really drink that much coffee (maybe a cup a day each), and half because we are trying to be pretty minimalist about the amount of *stuff* we have. (Oh, and also half because I am a bit OCD and don't like things on my counter tops.)

(Wait, how many halves is that? What are we at now, two wholes? Right. Like I said, math's not my thing. Did I even say that, ever? I'm saying it now: math is not my thing. The only way I was even able to get into university was to switch my French mark with my math mark—for some reason they let you do that here in Canada. But now I can't speak French very well either, so I'm doubly useless.... Anyway: IRRELEVANT.)

Where was I? Oh, OCD. Even the toaster oven being out on the counter bothers me, I am this close to hiding it in a cupboard and just bringing it out when we need it.

Does this make you think I'm crazy? Needless to say it makes Adam think I'm crazy.

He may have a point.

MY point here (and I swear I have one) is that we don't have a coffee maker but in the depths of this summer heat I have been starting to like iced coffee and lately have just been brewing it and then adding ice to it. (Wait, I *do* have a coffee maker. SORRY. My fabulous in-laws bought a little one cup deal when they were house-sitting for us once. So in case you're keeping track: No good at French, can't do math, and also a liar.)

Anyway, a while ago my dear friend Celene sent me the following recipe.

You don't need a coffee maker or even electricity. You just need ground coffee and a jar! Brilliant! And I've been drinking it nonstop ever since.

Like. . .nonstop. I've had three this morning. Iced coffees I mean.

OK, five.

Can you tell? (I'm so sorry.)

(I need to stop.)

(I can't stop. Help.)

YOU'LL NEED:

Jar

Fine sieve or coffee filter

⅓ cup ground coffee (medium-coarse grind is best)

Milk (I use almond milk. Because in addition to being a unilingual, math-inept liar, I am also a non-milk-drinking vegetarian. I *know.*)

A sweetener like sugar, honey, or agave nectar (optional)

DIRECTIONS

1. In a jar, stir together the coffee and 1½ cups water. Seal and let rest at room temperature overnight, or 12 hours.

2. Strain twice through the coffee filter or sieve.

3. In a tall glass filled with ice, mix equal parts coffee concentrate and milk. Add sugar/honey/agave nectar as desired.

Yield: Two drinks.

Playing around with the amount of milk will make the drink as strong or weak as you like. You can also blend the whole shebang if that's more your style.

ALL ABOUT ORGANICS

One of my biggest complaints about the new trendiness of the green movement is that it has left a huge chunk of the population out of the fun.

For those with a fixed income, low income, or no income at all (classifications that can encompass everyone from savvy seniors on a budget to ramen-swilling university students), buying trendy eco-products with the price tags to match is simply impossible. That's why so much of my philosophy involves simply doing it yourself and getting away from consuming altogether—most anything *truly* green and eco-friendly will be easier and cheaper than the alternative (especially since the greener option sometimes means just not buying something in the first place).

This is why I encourage people to make cleaning products instead of buying them, and to shop secondhand at every opportunity. The idea is not to replace consumption of polluting products with consumption of "green" products, but to reduce consumption, period.

Where this philosophy can run into a small hiccup is around the topic of food. Not everyone has the time, the space, or even the desire to grow their own food. (I'll readily cop to that last one after vowing to start a garden for three years running. Ask me how that's worked out. Actually, don't. Let's just forget I ever said anything—I'll do it next year, I *swear.*)

Even if you are someone who does have a deep-seated desire to get your hands dirty, many are limited by lack of space for a garden or by a horrendously short growing season.

Although I'll confess that I haven't yet gotten my own garden up and running due to a fatal combination of rental housing and procrastination, I did run a gardening program called G.R.O.W. (Gardening, Recycling, Organics, and Worms) during my five-year stint working with at-risk teens as a Youth Resource Worker. G.R.O.W. essentially consisted of my bribing teens to plant, grow, and harvest organic veggies to sell at our local farmers market.

Trying to encourage sometimes surly, usually lethargic teenagers to care about sustainability, the local food movement, and organic growing methods was an uphill battle at times, but I was always amazed at what we accomplished.

One of the most common conversations I had with my teens was about organic food. When they first began in the G.R.O.W. program, my informal surveys indicated that many felt eating organic produce was too expensive and a waste of money.

By the end of the summer, when they had seen firsthand how much labor it took to nurture veggies until they were ready for harvest, they would often want to charge five dollars for a zucchini or ten for a big butternut squash.

Besides being excellent price-gougers in training (probably destined for employment at some of the more upscale organic food markets), it was fascinating to see how their attitudes toward food changed as they became closer to the process. I'm not saying they immediately traded their big-gulps for kale smoothies, but healthy eating and organically grown foods seemed to make a little more sense when they were able to see things from the other side of the food-production chain.

And honestly, I can't say that I disagree with their earlier statements about the cost of healthy food. Our minds are funny that way. I have to admit that I'll sometimes balk at spending six dollars on a bag of organic oranges, but then find myself three hours later coughing up almost the equivalent for fancy coffee, without batting so much as an eyelash.

In the same vein, organic canned beans seem pricey at almost twice the price of normal beans, but one aisle over I'll eagerly spend the same amount on a bag of chips. One nourishes, one gives me caffeine anxiety. One is chock-full of protein and iron, one leaves tell-tale grease marks on my T-shirt. Which is worth more?

This isn't a pithy "latte-factor" thing where I tell you to give up your mochas and buy bok choy instead, but it is a reminder (to me too) to be conscious of our attitudes at the intersection of food and money, because they often make no sense when considered logically.

Food is more than something to shove in your mouth while watching *Jersey Shore.* Its main purpose is to fuel your body.

And yes, obviously organically grown food can be expensive, often more so than its conventionally grown cousin, but, when you're focused on saving a few bucks to get something that many argue is devoid of any actual nutritional content, what are you really buying except the satisfaction of eating your greens without any of the actual benefits of doing so?

Studies offer conflicting results to answer the question of whether conventionally grown and organic produce are comparable, nutritionally speaking, but most studies do seem to agree that vegetables grown today contain between 5 and 40 percent fewer vitamins and minerals than they did just fifty years ago.[11]

At play here is a pretty basic cause-effect scenario: Vegetables get their minerals from the soil they are grown in, but if that soil is devoid of minerals due to over-farming or repeatedly growing a single crop in the same area over a number of years, the vegetables too will be nutritionally empty. Organic growing methods typically emphasize crop rotation and replenishing soil nutrients, so buying organic produce does more than just contribute to your grocer's profits; it may be helping your spinach pack more of a nutritional punch.

I try to buy organic when I can, and I rationalize paying an increased price for our food by figuring that I save money by making my own cleaners and beauty products, not using my dryer, and avoiding one-time-use items like Ziplocs and wrapping paper. These choices enable me to free up a decent chunk of cash to buy food that will truly nourish me.

BUT, if you're not sold on organic on price or on principle, there are still some great alternatives to the supermarket.

Most cities now have at least one or two farmers markets. Besides being absolutely *incredible* for people watching, they provide vegetables that are often less expensive and fresher than they would be at the grocery store. It's also a poignant reminder to eat food that's in season. I've often found myself getting annoyed because I can't find any strawberries at my local market before realizing that it's not even June yet, and they're not ripe!

Buying from farmers markets allows you the opportunity to talk directly to the person in charge of planting, growing, and harvesting your food. You can ask questions, share recipes, and learn more than you ever wanted to know about their homegrown produce. The best part is that almost 100 percent of what you spend on farmers market produce is going directly to the farmer themselves, unlike shopping at a grocery store where farmers' profits are quickly eaten up by shipping, stocking, and overhead costs.

So, if you don't want to get your hands dirty (and honestly, *that's OK*, says the three-time non-gardener), it is still easy to take a few steps away from rushing through a crowded grocery store with a cart overloaded with plastic packages and move toward eating food that's fresh and local, and that supports the fantastic local men and women who make their livelihoods putting food on our tables.

QUICK TIP

Moving? Use clean sheets, pillowcases, and towels to pack breakable items like dishes and framed artwork. The soft material will help cushion your breakables, reducing or eliminating the need for bubble wrap. As an added bonus, linens and kitchen items are also usually among the first things you'll need to unpack at your new place, so using one to help pack the other means you'll find everything you need in one box.

Boho table settings

I can be a little weird sometimes. Like color-coding my books, nothing-on-my-countertops, mental-breakdown-when-the-shoes-aren't-lined-up-perfectly-by-the-door *weird*.

In my advanced age, however, I have come to embrace this weirdness to some degree, realizing that it is as much a part of me as my blue eyes, or that odd third bone in my ankle. Nonetheless, when I discover something that can temper this weirdness and loosen the white-knuckled death grip I have on the physical objects in my immediate surroundings, I am all for it (and if it involves thrift store shopping and old-lady china, all the better!).

The time has come to replace our dishes, which are old and chipped and missing at least six or seven plates and bowls. (I suspect some have made their way into Adam's truck, which is a black hole for coffee mugs and assorted clothing. Abandon all hope, ye who enter there.) (Also, watch your feet, you might step on an old burrito.) Unsurprisingly if you know anything about me at all, it has taken me a ridiculous time to pick out a new set.

I don't think I am alone in this constant quest for perfection, for a picture-perfect home or a perfectly laid table, but rather than comforting me, I am becoming aware that this solidarity simply means that there are legions of people out there obsessing about finding the perfect tableware that is cohesive without being overwhelmingly matchy-matchy, modern without being cold, practical without being ugly.

How many other people out there are having anxiety attacks trying to set the table? My god, it's exhausting.

Recently, however, I have discovered that going in the complete *opposite* direction has allowed me a surprising sense of relief, and I have saved a whack of cash too (the better to go secondhand clothes shopping with, my dear), so I am going to share it with you, fellow neurotic table-setters. I know you're out there!

Stop saving your pennies and lurking in department stores. Stop looking at china patterns and gravy boats. Be like Macklemore—go and pop some tags/ with just twenty dollars in your pocket./You'll be hunting, looking for some dishes/and it will be effing awesome.

Now, consistency and uniformity are not the goals here; an entire set of the same floral dishes screams elderly retiree having supper with her grandkids. An entire set of *mismatched* dishes, on the other hand, some with the aforementioned floral pattern, some pink, some blue, some with that awesome gold racing stripe—this screams laid back and vintage, a breezy style that belies one's crazy obsessive nature. Keeping the dishes approximately the same size helps create a pulled-together look, while the interplay of patterns and colors looks fabulous and bohemian. It's the table-setting equivalent of tying a kerchief around your head and smoking a hookah.

The best part is that this mismatched look works with pretty much any style, lending an unexpected punch of fun and whimsy to sleek modern interiors and fitting in perfectly with shabby chic.

Actually, I lied, the *best* part is that you can probably score an entire table setting for less than twenty dollars, *and* you're reusing, *and* you're saving all the packaging and waste from a new set, *and* you can stop going crazy over dishes. (Seriously. Stop it.)

When I started doing this, I asked each of my family members to find me a plate for my birthday. They each spent between twenty-five cents and two dollars (my mom has always been a high roller), and I ended up with the beginnings of my mismatched, quirky, Zooey-Deschanel-if-she-were-plates table setting.

I know that old-lady china is not everyone's cup of tea, so another option is to outfit your table with the any and all white dishes that you can dig up from your local secondhand store. Keeping it plain makes it easy to add pieces as you find them in secondhand stores or vintage shops without looking like you have a mish-mash of patterns. A thrifted collection of white dishes in different styles and sizes gives a relaxed, casual look, plus all the positive environmental benefits without the wild floral style.

If you still don't feel that eating off of vintage dishes is the best thing ever (and seriously, why not?), it can still be a great idea to pick up some secondhand plates to use for barbecues, kids parties, and other events where you'd typically use paper. The cost makes it practical to use in settings where you'd be worried about the safety of your regular dishes, and a mismatched set makes it easy to replace pieces that do end up breaking, or disappearing into a black hole to live cheek-to-cheek with an old burrito.

Simple food storage

OK, so you've made a delicious meal from natural ingredients, Instagrammed a picture of your food on sweet secondhand dishes, eaten said meal, and then washed up with earth-friendly dish soap. What are you going to do with the leftovers?

Doing such an amazing job at reducing the amount of waste packaging coming *into* your house is powerful motivation to avoid creating more waste going *out*. Unfortunately, repackaging and storing food is responsible for tons of waste generated by households in North America. The good news is that it's simple to change this.

I like to start by simply taking away the option to use throwaway packaging. If I don't have plastic wrap, paper towels, or zip-top plastic bags, I can't use them—or throw them away, for that matter.

Just like choosing not to buy junk food, I find that this is a decision easiest made in the aisles of the grocery store, rather than when I'm at home, in a hurry to get things packed away the easiest way possible.

In place of these items that were once essential in my kitchen, I've subbed in the following:

- Jars. So many jars. For salads, soups, sauces, juice, opened packages of things. Just jars. Lots of jars.
- Airtight glass containers for leftovers. I found that when I used plastic ones it was way too tempting to throw them out when I inevitably found them filled with leftovers of unknown origin, quietly growing fur at the back of my fridge. But if I've paid seven to ten dollars for a glass container, you're damn right I'm donning the hazmat gear to rescue it (or more likely, bribing Adam to do it).
- Aluminum foil is a great stand-in for plastic wrap and can be easily recycled or saved for reuse.
- Wax paper is great for wrapping sandwiches. So are reusable sandwich pouches you can make or purchase; many close with Velcro and are easy to launder or wipe clean.
- Reuse empty yogurt, sour cream, or cream cheese containers. You've already got them and you have to wash them before tossing them into the recycling bin anyway, so you may as well use them again.
- Invest in reusable lunch containers like bento boxes or tiffins to avoid waste when sending off your little one (or yourself) with a bagged lunch.

A young Canadian couple has created an awesome substitute for plastic wrap, called Abeego. Abeego is hemp and cotton fabric infused with a blend of beeswax, resin, and jojoba oil, making it flexible and able to stick to itself, seal bowls and wrap cheese. The fact that it is absolutely adorable doesn't hurt either. I've been using one of their sandwich wraps in Adam's lunch for almost a year now and it works like a hot damn, while creating zero waste and nixing the necessity for a clunky container. Check it out for yourself at www.abeego.ca

CHAPTER 5

Gardening

A WORD FROM THE GARDENING GURU IMPOSTER

I am far from an expert gardener. Most of my experience has been picked up through trial and error (and error and error) during my three-year stint running a gardening program with teenagers. We approached the subject of gardening as a sort of experiment with low expectations and little formal guidance, learning as we went, answering questions and solving problems as they arose.

This approach was decidedly unlike me, as I usually like to have things planned out right down to the letter, but I think it really was the best way we could have approached it. Sitting down and learning everything we needed to know would have seemed so daunting that I might not have ever gotten started in the first place, and hands-on learning will almost always be more attractive to teens than long-winded lectures.

Gardening, you see, can be as simple or as complicated as you make it. Don't be intimidated by thinking that you need to create some mammoth garden with eighteen different varieties of twenty different vegetables and an encyclopedic knowledge of fertilizers and pH levels before you begin. In its most basic form all you need to grow your own food is dirt, a plant, water, and sunshine. It can be that simple!

My status as a novice gardener is important to mention, not only to assuage my fear of being chased down the street by a gang of irate green-thumbed horticulturalists and outed as some sort of gardening guru imposter, but also to reassure you that you don't need to know much to begin. Honestly. If you have the desire and the will and the time and the space, you can garden. Simple as that.

Planting a vegetable garden is a great way to make better use of your lawn, as well as reconnect with the earth, save money, reduce waste, spend more time outside, and get exercise too.

So let's say you're ready to go green in the most literal sense of the word. Where do you start?

Deciding to begin a garden can be overwhelming if you dive in head-first, armed with seed catalogs and fertilizer, resolving to never again eat anything that you didn't coax from the soil with your very own two hands.

Do this, and I can almost guarantee that, come late August, your friends will find you miserable, overwhelmed, and suffering from a near-fatal zucchini overdose. (Pro gardening tip: one zucchini plant does not equal one zucchini. One zucchini plant equals approximately eighty-six zucchini. So don't plant five plants. For example. Not that anyone would do that. Especially not me.)

Remember when you wanted to transition to natural cleaning products and I was all "Hey guys! Whoa! Slow down!"? I advised against a grand dramatic overhaul then, and I am doing the same now, because as satisfying as it is to simply charge ahead full bore and make BIG! CHANGES!, this approach isn't terribly conducive to long-term success. So the key here is temperance and moderation.

Start small, and grow.

Here's how.

MAKE IT

Herb garden

If you are a complete novice to the strange and wonderful world of gardening, start with herbs. Growing your own fresh herbs is inexpensive, dead simple, and the quickest way to get your hands dirty and instantly gain some gardening street cred.

Purchasing a small herb plant often costs the same as buying cut herbs in the grocery store, so even if this little experiment crashes and burns (*which it won't! probably!*) you really can't lose.

If your grocery store sells potted herbs, pick up a few of your favorites next time you're replenishing your pantry, or head down to your local garden center to browse their selection. When you bring your little plants home you can either keep the herbs in their plastic pots on a windowsill, or transplant them into a nice planter with good drainage to keep on your porch or balcony.

One thing to note is that anything in the mint family should be kept in a container separate from other plants as it can quickly overrun your entire garden, but the rest is just as you would expect: water as needed, harvest often, and boom! Little tasty plants that you are singlehandedly keeping alive!

Yes, you! You with the black thumb of death!

Fresh herbs are the culinary gift that just keeps on giving. Garnishing your meals with the good homegrown stuff (and then proudly announcing to your dinner guests that you have done so) saves you from having to buy them prepackaged every week at the supermarket, makes you look like a domestic goddess, and is also, incidentally, a great way to objectively evaluate your commitment to gardening.

You see, starting off with a few tiny pots of herbs is kind of like when your parents made you get a goldfish before letting you have a puppy. If your basil is limp and shriveled after only two weeks, you may well decide that becoming a loyal farmers market shopper is a better fit for you (and that's entirely OK!). If, however, your herbs flourish and you swell with pride and wholesome delight, then you can move on to frying bigger fish. Which is not fish at all, of course, but vegetables.

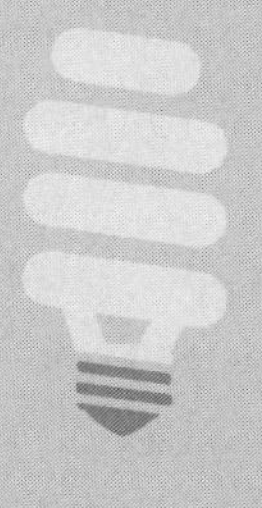

QUICK TIP

Harvest your herbs often to prevent your plants from becoming overgrown or going to seed. If you have more herbs than you know what to do with, consider building up a stash of dried herbs by tying up small bunches with string, and hanging them upside down until dry. Alternately, finely chop herbs and freeze them in an ice cube tray filled with olive oil. When it comes time to cook, just add one or two herbed oil cubes to the pan for a burst of fresh flavor.

Salad garden

One step above growing your own herbs is planting a small salad garden. It's a perfect option for both gardening novices and apartment dwellers with tiny balconies that don't seem good for much else.

The best way to go about this is to find yourself a large planter pot (preferably not plastic) and plant a variety of seedlings from the lettuce family—a mix of radicchio, spinach, mustard greens, arugula, and butter leaf lettuce is a great start, but customize the plants to your taste.

When it comes time to harvest your goodies, just snip the bigger leaves off from the outside of the plant. By harvesting as you go, you will have access to a constantly replenishing source of fresh greens, without ever having to replant.

Although it's a teensy bit more intense than growing herbs (I mean, we're talking about an appetizer now, not just a garnish), growing a salad garden is still very forgiving of beginners. It's contained, it's simple, and you can even drag the whole operation indoors come fall.

Being able to cut a bunch of fresh greens for a simple supper salad is a sweet, eco-friendly way to begin a simple meal, and it also helps avoid food waste by letting you replenish your salad supply on an as-needed basis.

There's nothing more humbling than that moment when you discover a head of slimy lettuce at the back of your crisper drawer, forgotten because you meant to make a salad yesterday but ended up eating popcorn for dinner instead.

Oops.

Real live vegetable garden

Now the fun begins!

Up to this point all the serious gardeners have been rolling their eyes and laughing at our twee discussions of herb gardens and salad greens, but as we are getting around to the good stuff I can almost feel them rolling up their sleeves and getting ready to dig in.

(See what I did there? Gardening humor!)

Since the whole point of growing your own vegetables is to be able to eat those same vegetables, I think one of the best ways to decide what to plant in your garden is to think about your favorite meals and use their ingredients as a guide. There's really no sense in having a boomer crop of tomatoes if you're sort of *meh* about the taste.

If, on the other hand, you are hungry for results and just want to grow something—anything!—and would like to engineer a somewhat foolproof entry into the gardening world, here are some of the easiest vegetables to grow:

- Beans
- Kale
- Squash
- Carrots
- Radishes
- Tomatoes
- Zucchini
- Lettuce

After you've chosen five to ten different vegetables, it's time to take a trip down to your local garden center.

No, no, I said the *local* one, not the big-box store staffed with well-intentioned individuals who—bless their hearts—couldn't tell an annual from a perennial if their lives depended on it. They won't be any help to us. I mean, *we* can't tell an annual from a perennial either! Sometimes we don't even remember which is which. (Perennial: *what does it mean?!*)

Clearly we need help, and going to a big-box store would be like asking the blind to lead the blind.

No, we amateurs need a kindly old gardening fanatic, someone who can take us by the hand and take us by the heart, someone to show us that one magic type of heritage tomato that can grow like a weed in our sandy soil. We need a feisty gal with a green thumb who can intelligently debate the merits of spinach vs. Swiss chard, the uses and abuses of fertilizer, and the strange, beautiful world of companion planting.

If you spend a few minutes befriending the staff at your local garden center it will go a long way toward ensuring the success of your garden. These folks (and if anyone can be referred to as "folks," it is *these folks*) are absolutely invaluable, because they live where you live.

More than any book or manual or TV show or famous gardening guru, they know what it takes to garden where you want to garden. They know the soil, the climate, the growing season, and probably even the phases of the moon if you manage to get your hands on that rare gem, a hippie gardener.

Local gardening gurus know when it's safe to plant and what other gardeners are doing, they have made mistakes and grown success stories, and they are happy—so happy!—to share all this knowledge with you. All you have to do is ask.

When comparing the merits of large chain stores vs. local establishments, it's easy to get seduced by gardening tools that cost a few dollars less, or seed aisles that offer twice the selection. It's easy to feel like you're saving money, but what you're actually doing is missing out on an incredible wealth of knowedge that is in rapid danger of going extinct if it's not passed on.

Once you are at your local garden center I recommend buying seedlings, which are baby plants. It's tempting to buy seeds, not only because they are less expensive, but also because you might not feel like you are *really* gardening unless you start from scratch. Some hardcore gardening snobs might agree, but as someone who has been (and let's face it, *still* is) in the first, scared, tentative stage of gardening, I find that planting seedlings offers a greater chance of success, as well as providing a delightful feeling of instant gratification that planting seeds alone just can't match.

QUICK TIP

Buy organic heritage seedlings whenever you can. Most fruits and vegetables have an incredibly diverse range of varieties, but we typically only see one or two different kinds in the grocery store. By choosing to grow heritage plants we can preserve that diversity and give a big green thumbs down to monoculture.

When you start with seedlings, just a few hours spent digging in the dirt can transform your plot from a barren patch of earth to a real live garden! With plants and everything! The garden will look terribly convincing right off the bat and this is just the sort of inspiration that will continue to keep you going—as well as be a great boon to the tender ego of the amateur gardener.

To figure out how to space your seedlings, it has always helped me to set them on the ground, still in their pots, approximately where they are to be planted. This way I can adjust spacing and coordinate any companion planting I am planning on doing (more on that in a minute). Most seedlings will come with a plant marker specifying the suggested spacing between plants. Use this and any advice from your local gardening guru to plan out and plant your vegetable garden. (For a few different ideas of where to plant your garden, check out the raised garden beds section coming up next.)

After you plant them, give the plants a good soak, sit back, and admire your efforts. I'll look the other way if you want to take a few selfies in front of your peas. You've earned it.

You have just planted your first vegetable garden! Be honest, don't you feel a little bit proud of yourself? No matter how long you've thought about doing it, or how many times you started and gave up, or how many dead houseplants it took to get you here—you DID it!

You proved everyone wrong—even your brother who laughed mightily when you told him your plans, reminding you that you couldn't even keep your childhood pet gerbil alive, at which point you became irate and screamed that it was HIS gerbil who ATE your gerbil and then escaped. Really, who could have predicted that sort of cannibalism? It was a tragic incident impossible to foresee, and even if it *could* have been prevented, the onus would have been on YOU, Liam, to stop your gerbil's cannibalistic tendencies.

I say it here in black and white: I have a clean conscience in the matter of The Great Gerbil Catastrophe of 1992.

(RIP, Shrubby.)

Anyway! Gardening, like most things in life that are unfamiliar and strange, can be daunting to begin. But when I started out, armed with little more than a box of dirt and a few seedlings, I liked to remind myself what an incredible privilege it was to be able to grow our own food.

Many do not have that privilege, many would give *anything* for the ability to do what you are doing. So take a few moments to sit—with aching shoulders and dirt under your nails—and be grateful for your small patch of land. Send a few thoughts of gratitude for your little seedlings standing hopefully in the rich dark earth, for the vegetables you will soon be eating, and especially for the fact that you got a book published before your brother did, so that the world might learn the truth about your childhood gerbil once and for all.

While you are on this gardening adventure, be open to learning—because picking up new skills and learning from your mistakes is just as valuable as having a successful garden right off the bat. When you make mistakes—as you assuredly will—you can just rip everything out at the end of the season and start fresh next year.

It is incredibly therapeutic to be able to wipe the slate clean and try again. Zen, almost.

Growing your own food eliminates an enormous amount of pollution—you are making a conscious choice to do away with unnecessary transportation, pesticides, and packaging. You are given the opportunity to dig deep, get your hands dirty, and reconnect with the process of planting, growing, and harvesting. It's an important process, a lost process, and one that is especially valuable for children.

There's also the small bonus that serving a meal made up entirely of things you've grown in your own garden means ultimate green-thumb bragging rights.

Raised garden beds

While we were talking about planting your vegetables, you might have been wondering where, exactly, you'd be doing that. If you have land and you are aiming your sights a bit higher than salad and garnishes, one of the easiest ways to get started is with a raised garden bed.

These have been popping up everywhere, from community gardens to suburban backyards, and they have become hugely popular because they offer somewhat of a closed system. You can build the frame, set it on a few layers of newspaper weed barrier (find out how to make it on page 152), fill the whole thing with soil and compost, and know that nothing will end up in your garden except what you put in it. This is especially helpful for areas with depleted or weedy soil, as you will start off on the right foot with a nutrient-rich, weed-free growing environment.

You will require some basic carpentry skills to create a raised garden bed, and if you're not particularly adept with a hammer this can be a great opportunity to employ the Beg/Barter/Borrow system talked we about in Chapter 3. Promise someone a cut of your harvest if they'll do the grunt work for you; most people would be delighted to donate a few hours of their time in exchange for homegrown produce throughout the summer.

The size of the frame is up to you, but I find that building it so that you can easily access the entire bed without having to step into it makes for the easiest setup. To this end, make it no more than one to two feet high, and no wider than four feet across for adults—and three feet across if you'll have little hands digging alongside you. The length of the bed is often dependent upon how much room you have and how many plants you are planning to grow, but I find that somewhere between eight and twelve feet tends to be perfect.

When sourcing materials for your garden bed frame, don't be afraid to get creative. I have seen raised beds made out of everything from plain ol' store-bought two-by-fours to elaborately upcycled shutters—even old bathtubs. By all means indulge your ingenuity and let your Pinterest-loving-self take the reins, but use caution when selecting the wood, and avoid anything pretreated or pressure-treated, as the chemicals used in this sort of preparation can leach into your soil. This, unfortunately, excludes the darling of DIY-ers everywhere: pallets.

I know, I KNOW! Pallets owe their popularity to the fact that they are cheap (or free!), easily attainable, and charmingly rustic. However, most pallets should only be used outside, and definitely not where they will be in contact with food, small children or pets. The wood used to make pallets is often heat-treated or pressure treated and sometimes fumigated to repel insects. You don't want to go to all the trouble of creating a pesticide-free garden and then have your trendy pallets poisoning the soil.

(Don't worry, you don't have to abandon them altogether—they're great for creating vertical gardens of ornamental plants like succulents, or making outdoor furniture, but unless you know for sure that the wood hasn't been treated, it really is best to steer clear of their use in vegetable gardens.)

When you've found your materials of choice and cut them to size, create a rectangular frame for the border of the garden bed and secure it together with screws or nails. For extra stability, attach a few small posts to the inner frame, extending six to ten inches below the bottom of the frame itself. To anchor these into the ground, dig holes in the corresponding depth and location of the posts, place your garden bed frame with the posts in the holes and tightly pack soil around the post edges. This added step will help stabilize your frame and prevent it from shifting against the weight of its contents.

This whole process is fairly simple, but if you don't feel up to it, don't let the construction of a raised garden bed deter you from getting started. If you would prefer to skip the raised beds altogether, just go old school and dig out a garden right into the ground.

There are a few simple tips that you can use to make your life a little easier when going this route. If you plan ahead by a few months, you can place cardboard, a tarp or some other heavy, light-blocking material on the area you're planning to convert to garden space.

Weigh the material down with heavy rocks or buckets, and if you're using cardboard or newspaper make sure to keep it damp. After a few months, the lack of sunlight and air circulation will have killed or weakened pretty much everything underneath, making it a snap to quickly weed, turn, and get ready for planting come spring.

One thing to keep in mind is that creating an in-ground garden might require a little more attention to soil composition, since you will be working with the dirt already present in your garden area. Consider bringing a small sample into your local garden center to test the pH, and add compost and manure to enrich the soil if necessary.

A pesticide-free garden

One of the reasons that organic produce can be a bit more expensive than conventionally grown produce is their lower crop yields, due in part to the absence of pesticides. Not spraying fruits and vegetables with pesticides can leave fruits and vegetables vulnerable to pests, and may result in partial crop loss.

Considering this, why even go pesticide-free in the first place? Well it seems a bit silly to put so much time into selecting, planting and growing your gorgeous vegetables, only to turn around and spray them with low-grade poison every week. Washing fruits and vegetables does remove some pesticide residue, but what leaches into the ground water and is absorbed by the roots then goes into the produce you're serving for dinner—if you wouldn't drink diluted pesticides, why would you eat them?

So let's talk about how to achieve a pesticide-free garden.

My favorite way to create a garden that is both pesticide- *and* pest-free is by working with nature, not against it. Instead of beginning a season-long campaign of chemical warfare, we can enlist plants to do our dirty work for us through a process called companion planting. This involves buddying up your plants so that they benefit each other by adding nutrients to the soil, providing favorable growing conditions and, yes, repelling common pests.

I mean, could it get any more incredible?

Companion planting also has the added benefit of adding color to your garden by interspersing occasional rows of flowers in with your leafy greens.

Here's a quick and dirty guide to my favorite companion plants to add to your garden, partially adapted from West Coast Seeds.[12, 13]

- **Catnip**—Attracts pollinators and repels aphids, flea beetles, Japanese beetles, ants, weevils, and squash bugs.
- **Cilantro**—Repels aphids, potato beetles, and spider mites.
- **Chrysanthemum**—White-flowering chrysanthemums repel Japanese beetles.
- **Clover**—A great all-around companion plant that attracts many beneficial elements. Plant near cabbage to deter cabbage worms.
- **Lupin**—Attracts honeybees and fixes nitrogen in the soil, helping fertilize plants naturally.
- **Marigolds**—A great companion for all plants, particularly peppers and tomatoes; repels many pests, including nematodes and beet-leaf hoppers.
- **Nasturtium**—These pretty flowers trap aphids; deter whiteflies and cucumber beetles; and attract predatory insects like spiders, which eat other pests. (As an added bonus, nasturtium flowers are edible and can be added to salads for a burst of delicious color.)
- **Sage**—Plant near carrots to repel the carrot moth and rust fly, but don't plant near cucumbers.
- **Sunflowers**—When planted near corn, sunflowers are said to increase corn yields.

To simplify the companion-planting process, I usually start off by alternating rows of marigolds and nasturtiums with my vegetables, then planting appropriate pest-deterring plants as needed throughout the growing season (e.g., If I noticed that I was overrun with Japanese beetles, I'd add catnip).

Seed storing

If you have chosen to grow organic or heirloom vegetables you may want to save their seeds to plant next year. By doing this you are completing the circle of life that we learned about in that most classic of films, *The Lion King*. *Nants ingonyama bagithi baba*, *Sithi uhhmm ingonyama!*

(Did you know that those are the lyrics to the beginning of the song "The Circle of Life"? The language is Zulu, and I had no idea that's what they were until I just looked it up. I always thought it was something like *ahh Sabena*. . .*wa wa deet jojoba, Mm hmm hmm hey.* Go figure! I mean to heck with the seeds, I think we've all learned something really important here today!)

Anyway. To grow from a seed and then be returned to seed once more—what could be more perfect? I think dear old Rafiki would be proud.

Doing this with grocery store produce usually won't usually work, as many conventionally grown fruits and vegetables are either hybrid varieties or have been genetically modified to be sterile—the seeds simply won't grow. Don't you find that sort of heartbreaking? No circle of life for all those supermarket apples and green peppers piled in shiny little pyramids, just a short flat line ending in a period. Full stop.

For organic or heirloom fruits and vegetables, however, storing seeds is a great way to reduce your start-up expenses for next year—by that time you

may just be bold enough to start growing from seed!—as well as carrying on any plant varieties that were particularly successful for you this year.

The process is as simple as you'd think: collect the seeds from the fruit or vegetable that you'd like to save and lay them to dry on a sheet of newspaper. If you're doing a few different varieties at once, label the newspaper so they don't get mixed up.

Dry your seeds for about a week, then stick them in a paper envelope and label it with the type of plant and the date. Seeds should be kept cool and dry, so storing seed packets in a sealed jar on a basement shelf is perfect.

Seeds will last roughly three years from the date you stored them. If you want to test to see if seeds are viable (which is a good idea if you're not sure they're not hybrid varieties and want to check their viability before going to the trouble of drying and storing them), take about ten seeds and sandwich them between two layers of damp newspaper or paper towel. Keep the newspaper/towel in a sealed bag in a warm location and check daily to see if any seeds have sprouted.

After a week count the number of sprouts. If the germination rate is around 80 percent or higher, the seeds you saved should be good to plant. If not, you may be better off starting fresh or planting extra seeds to compensate for those that won't grow.

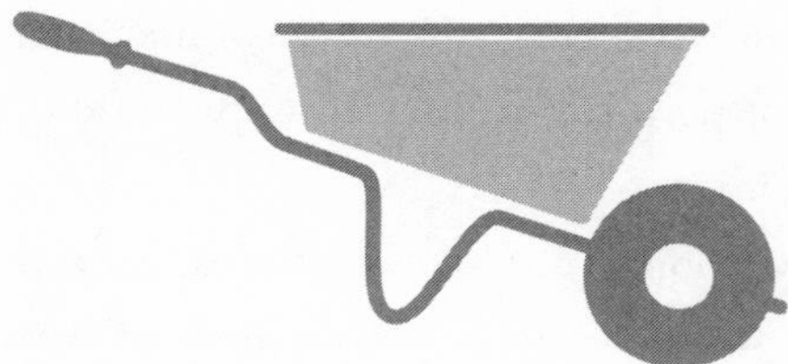

Start composting

Choosing to compost vegetable peels, table scraps, and spoiled food is a simple way to reduce waste, restore soil nutrient levels, and enrage your partner (more on that later).

The how is just as simple as the why: in its most basic form you can compost by simply depositing kitchen waste in a designated corner of your yard and calling it a day, but doing so may attract vermin, and most people in residential settings prefer to contain the pile somehow so they look like environmentalists rather than hoarders.

Pre-made compost bins are available to purchase at many hardware stores—try to support a local business if possible—or you can make one if you are handy with power tools.

Your compost bin will be holding decomposing garbage, so it doesn't have to be pretty, but if you plan on using the compost in a food garden, don't use treated wood in its construction because the chemicals used might contaminate the soil.

You want to create a container large enough that you can turn the contents with a shovel or pitchfork to promote aeration, and you'll need a lid so you can deposit new compost and keep out rain and vermin. A small door at the bottom comes in handy when it comes time to remove your winnings, and ventilation along the sides aids in breaking down organic matter.

To start composting, keep a small bucket handy in your kitchen and use it to collect vegetable peels, cores, and pits, as well as any produce that has expired or gone moldy. Empty the bucket into your compost bin at the end of each day, and keep odors and fruit flies at bay by covering each addition of food waste with a layer of garden waste, like grass clippings or leaves. This can also help to reduce animal interest in your new backyard addition.

A good mix of green matter (fruit and vegetable waste) to supply nitrogen and brown matter (grass clippings, leaves, etc.) to provide carbon will ensure an environment ideal for decomposition. Bear in mind that composting is about as far from instant gratification as you can get—it will take anywhere from four months to a year to begin seeing that pile of peels and leaves turn into rich black soil. But in the meantime you are reducing waste and allowing food to break down and return to the earth as nature intended, instead of sealing it in plastic and sending it to the landfill.

All this—plus passively creating what gardeners refer to as "black gold," that rich, fertile soil for your garden—for free!

If you're in an apartment or condo, don't think that you have to miss out on the fun. Many cities have begun municipal composting programs. (And some even have curbside pickup! Lucky.)

Aaaand if you're not lucky enough to have such a forward-thinking local government, there's always worm composting.

Worms? What?! Who said that?

Worm compost

Hi, I'm Madeleine and I once kept a box of worms in my kitchen (Does that surprise you?)

Here's the deal: if you can't have an outdoor compost bin, it's really simple to create an indoor one, and it's nowhere near as messy, stinky, or gross as you might think.

But it does involve worms.

Instead of having an outdoor compost bin, you have one indoors. And instead of leaving the decomposition process to its own devices, you speed it up a bit by employing a tremendously hardworking wriggly little workforce.

To create a worm compost bin of your very own you can purchase a kit online or from some garden centers, or make one yourself.

To make, start with a large opaque 8–10 gallon rubber bin with a lid. Drill ten to twenty holes along the bottom, sides, and top for ventilation and drainage, then add a layer of shredded newspaper one or two inches thick, about half a cup of water to soak the newspaper, and approximately a pound of red wriggler worms (sometimes available at local bait shops).

Place another bin or a tray underneath to catch any liquid runoff (which can be combined with equal amounts of water to make a rich fertilizer for houseplants), and presto! Vermiculture!

Now that you've gone and opened this can o' worms (sorry) your wriggly little friends can get to work eating and breaking down fruit and vegetable scraps into a rich, nutrient-dense byproduct. (OK, it's worm poop. But rich, nutrient-dense byproduct sounded better.)

Much as you would in a backyard compost bin, add a layer of shredded newspaper or leaves each time you add organic matter. This will do a lot to prevent fruit flies, absorb excess moisture, and eliminate any odors.

Start slowly, as it will take a while for your worms to grow and reproduce to the point that they can handle compost from a whole family. A worm compost is a fascinating project to take on with small children, especially when it comes time to harvest the soil.

To harvest, choose a bright, warm, sunny day, head outside with a tarp and dump the contents of the bin.

Form several medium sized pyramid shaped piles on the tarp and leave them for fifteen or twenty minutes—the worms will try to avoid the sun by wriggling toward the center of the soil pyramids, at which point you can scoop off the top and add it to a bag or bucket for use in your garden.

Form more pyramids from the remaining soil and continue until you are left with a wriggling pile of worms. Add a fresh layer of moistened shredded newspaper to your bin, replace the worms and marvel over your bag of rich dark soil.

Things you CAN put in worm bins and outdoor composts:

- Fruit and vegetable peels
- Tea bags
- Coffee grounds
- Breads and grains
- Dryer lint
- Paper towels
- Unbleached shredded newspapers/cardboard
- Grass clippings/leaves

Things you can NOT put in worm bins and outdoor composts:

- Meat and dairy products
- Fats and oils like butter or olive oil
- Too many citrus fruits/onions (makes soil too acidic)
- Weeds/invasive plants
- Pet or human waste
- Corn dogs, Doritos, Funions and other non-foods

QUICK TIP

Give up the bottled water. Please? Not only is it ridiculously overpriced and horrifically wasteful, but it fails to offer any benefit over tap water. Many brands draw their water from a municipal supply—as in, the same water that comes out of your tap *for free.*

Additionally, bottled water companies aren't held to the same stringent standards as public waterworks. And, adding final insult to injury, plastic bottles can often leach harmful chemicals into the water and then languish in landfills for thousands of years if not properly recycled.[14]

It's better for everyone involved if you carry a jar or reusable water bottle to fill up instead.

Weed killer

Now that we've spent so much time learning how to grow things, let's talk about how to kill them!

I am *way* better at this part.

As much as we love Mother Nature, it is not an unconditional sort of love. While some of her creations earn her a standing ovation—the sun, all those cool clear lakes perfect for swimming, and of course, my man Ryan Gosling—other parts of nature are almost universally loathed, and weeds unfortunately fall into the latter category.

I'm of the opinion that manicured lawns are best left to golf courses, and even then I have to stifle an overwhelming urge to unbutton the view with a wild smattering of wildflowers (how whimsical!). If high-maintenance lawn maintenance is your thing, though, I can get on board with that and do what I can to offer some tips and tricks to help you achieve the lawn of your dreams in an eco-friendly way.

First up, the scourge of suburbia: Dandelions.

The best way to get rid of these common weeds is simply to pull them up by the roots. This is surprisingly satisfying, and also oddly fascinating when you see just how far down, and how *huge* some of the root systems are. Once you see that, their persistence and tenacity in the face of conventional weed sprays makes far more sense.

There are several fancy tools designed specifically to remove weeds along with a good chunk of their root systems, so avail yourself of one if it would make your life easier, but I've always just gone old school and thrown on a good pair of gardening gloves to pull those behemoths out one by one.

After you have completed this task and your lawn is full of gaping holes where dandelions used to be, take a jug of pickling vinegar (which has a slightly higher concentration of acetic acid than the normal kind) and pour a splash or two into the dandelion-hole. This vinegar bath helps to kill the root system and ensures that the dandelion won't simply grow back in a day or two.

You can repeat the vinegar bath over the course of a few days, then fill in the holes with fresh soil, and seed with the grass seed of your choice.

QUICK TIP

If all that weeding has made you hungry, you can use your weed pile to whip up a scrumptious salad (and how very Game of Thrones of you to feast upon your enemy!)

Dandelion greens make a fantastic (and free) salad base if you pick them early enough that the leaves are still tender. Just pick, rinse, and add to your favorite salad, but remember that dandelion leaves should be consumed only if you don't use pesticides or fertilizers on your lawn. Cheers!

As for the weeds that stubbornly poke up in between sidewalk cracks and paving stones, the most effective natural remedy I've found to date is boiling water.

It's free, non-toxic, and as easy as it sounds.

Pick a sunny day and boil a large pot of water. Once it has boiled, carefully carry it outside and pour the water directly over the weeds you'd like to eliminate. The boiling water will kill the weeds immediately, and when they dry you can simply sweep away their shriveled husks—no back-breaking weed pulling required!

Huzzah!

Weed barrier

For weeds that pop up in flower beds and other landscaped areas, using vinegar or boiling water isn't a great solution as it can often result in the death of innocent plant bystanders, so in these cases a more delicate solution is required.

Likewise, manually pulling weeds is a simple and effective method, but in areas like a landscaped garden bed, laying down a weed barrier is a better idea for long-term results.

Weed barriers made of cloth or plastic can be purchased at most garden centers, but if you dig into your recycling bin you can easily find the materials to make one yourself for free.

Find a stack of old newspapers, and head out to the area that you are desperate to transform into a weed-free zone. Carpet the area in layers of newspaper at least six to eight sheets deep, with generous overlaps between sheets.

Using a hose, soak the newspaper and then cover it completely with one or two inches of soil, mulch, or decorative stones—whatever you fancy. The newspaper will form a natural weed barrier, it won't cost you much more than the price of a thick Sunday edition, AND your garden will look all fancy-schmancy without taking a toll on Mother Nature.

QUICK TIP

If you're tired of the constant mow/water/fertilize/mow cycle of your lawn, consider getting rid of it altogether. It's not as bizarre as it sounds. Some water conservationists estimate that up to 40 percent of a household's water usage during the summer months is spent on outdoor watering, so ditching the lawn altogether can save you time, money, *and* a precious resource.

One eco-friendly option is to replace all that turf with plants indigenous to your region, which will require less water and—in my humble hippie opinion—look far prettier than any plain ol' square of green grass every could.

As an added bonus, on those balmy summer nights you can sit admiring your beautifully landscaped yard while sipping a mojito, as all around you your neighbors sweat behind the handle of a lawn mower, continuing their Sisyphean task.

Cheers!

CHAPTER 6

Relationships

WHAT TO DO WHEN YOUR PARTNER IS A SOUL-SUCKING PLANET KILLER

To say that my husband and I are quite different is perhaps the greatest understatement in the history of any understatement, ever.

Adam is an incredible athlete; I can't even catch a set of keys tossed my way in a generous underhand. Conversely, I'm a voracious reader who can usually be found with my nose buried between the musty pages of a thick novel, whereas he once gestured to our shelves crammed with books and announced proudly to my sister, "I haven't read *any* of these!"

These quirky little "opposites attract" anecdotes may seem like the perfect fodder for a kicky little odd-couple style sitcom, but in reality it can make for an exasperating series of United Nations-style negotiations about the smallest, most trivial decisions in our lives. Perhaps not surprisingly given our many differences, Adam is sometimes less than enthusiastic about my latest great idea for eco-friendly endeavors.

Our most recent marital tug of war was about composting. I have been a vegetarian for over ten years and, as you may guess, I generate a fair bit of vegetable waste. We don't own our house, and we live in an area where bears regularly stroll through our backyard looking for a midnight snack, so unfortunately an outdoor compost is out of the question.

Before I discovered worm composting, and not being satisfied with continuing to send perfectly good compost material to our local landfill, I soon discovered that our town provided a bin for compost at our recycling center, right next to those designated for cardboard, glass, etc. (Yours might too!)

Excited to begin this new phase in earth-friendly living, I began to keep my vegetable trimmings instead of tossing them. But, because I detest fruit flies and live in fear of discovering a colony of them breeding in my compost scraps, I decided to keep those vegetable scraps in our freezer.

Adam, funnily enough, objected to me keeping "garbage" in our freezer, and his objections were exacerbated by the fact that I wasn't always the most punctual about taking it to the recycling depot.

So for a while our routine looked like this: I would fill the freezer with bags of compost, feeling smugly satisfied that I was so drastically cutting down on our garbage waste (we were even able to downsize our garbage pail to one-third of its size). Meanwhile, as I was busy patting myself on the back, the compost would pile up until Adam would all of a sudden get so irate at having to dig under four bags of frozen vegetable peelings to get to the ice cube trays, that he would throw the whole thing in the garbage in a fit of rage.

So I guess I wasn't truly composting, I was just separating and freezing my food scraps before throwing them out. And enraging my husband.

I give this example partly to shame myself into taking the compost to the depot sooner (seriously Madeleine, *get it together!*) and partly to illustrate that we do not live in a perfect world where our partners/siblings/roommates always jump on board 100 percent with whatever insane hippie idea we come up with, whether it be something simple like recycling or a more dramatic endeavor like getting rid of the family car.

Having domestic disputes over frozen compost isn't something typically addressed in most eco-books, but I can't be the only one experiencing these issues—right?

What I discovered is sometimes we need to take a breath, put on our grown-up pants, and recognize that we can only change our own behavior.

It's wonderful to become the voice initiating positive change, whether it is in a workplace, a shared accommodation, or a romantic partnership, but if you tread too heavily you risk becoming *that person.* You know, the eco-warrior-soapbox-preacher that we all try to avoid because any conversation inevitably comes around to just what, *exactly,* you are doing wrong to ensure a barren, garbage-strewn wasteland of a world to pass down to future generations.

This is lame and depressing. Even if it is true, ain't nobody got time for that!

Seriously, don't be that guy.

The key approaches to remember are to 1) just do you, and 2) explore your options.

If you've started recycling in an attempt to edge toward a more eco-friendly lifestyle, you get a giant gold star, but you also have to recognize that others might not be as enthusiastic as you are. For your sanity and that of those around you, just do you. Offer the opportunity to others, but either focus on making sure you're recycling your stuff, or commit yourself to garbage picking in order to rescue recyclables from the trash. There's no shame in it either way. I've done both.

Gentle reminders are OK. Lectures and loud, passive-aggressive sighs when you spot soda cans in the trash are not.

Recognize the difference between educating people with your eco-knowledge and answering a question that was never asked in the first place. (If you're not sure which of these approaches you currently embody, see the quiz entitled "Are You an Insufferable Enviro-Nag?" on page 160).

Deciding to just do you is important because nothing is more annoying than being judged by anyone, for anything. None of us is perfect, not even you.

If you become a preacher you risk accomplishing the exact opposite of what you set out to do, because you will become so incredibly, insufferably self-righteous that those around you will delight in sabotaging your mission for little more than the exquisite pleasure of seeing your head explode when you find all those carefully collected bags of compost sitting innocently in your garbage can (*for example*).

If you have taken the quiz on page 160 and are absolutely certain that you aren't preaching, and those around you *still* aren't falling in with your plans to save the world, it might be time to explore your options. Why is this happening?

For example, let's revisit that little compost situation we had going on. One might, upon discovering the aforementioned compost bags in the garbage, ~~scream~~ politely inquire why a certain individual hates Mother Nature SO much that he is actively undermining all your efforts to do good. The individual in question might reply tersely that he doesn't have a problem with Mother Nature or with the compost itself, but with *someone* storing *garbage* in his *freezer*.

At this point, one would be remiss if one didn't point out that compost isn't garbage*, idiot*, and isn't that the whole point? Here your ~~opponent~~ partner might set his jaw a little tighter, continue playing video games, and refuse to reply to any further questions.

That, my friends, is how you know that you have ~~won~~ made significant progress.

Just what has all this friendly, open communication accomplished? Well, several things actually.

First of all, you get the bed to yourself tonight.

More importantly, you now know that, while this infuriating individual is most certainly guilty of many (many) things, being against composting isn't one of them—he merely objects to the compost cluttering up the freezer.

Now that you have identified the problem, you have plenty of time (perhaps whilst greedily luxuriating alone in your queen-sized bed) to figure out a creative way to remedy the situation. Personally, I decided to make it my mission to get the compost to the recycling center before it could be thrown out, but obviously the solution will be different for every situation.

After some gentle investigation you might discover that your office mates aren't recycling because the recycling bin is in an inconvenient location or improperly labeled, or because they are unsure of what they can toss in. Perhaps your roommate is avoiding your natural cleaning solutions in favor of his favorite Toxic Bleach-Spray because he hates the smell of the tea tree oil you add.

Most people are good, and most people want to do good. If you make eco-friendly choices easy, accessible, and user-friendly, chances are that most people will happily jump aboard your bandwagon.

QUIZ: ARE YOU AN INSUFFERABLE ENVIRO-NAG?

Take this highly scientific quiz to answer this question once and for all.

Place a check mark next to each statement that is true for you (BE HONEST).

HAVE YOU EVER...

- ❏ Recycled?
- ❏ Upcycled?
- ❏ Composted?
- ❏ Bragged about composting?
- ❏ Berated a small child for wasting paper with their "art" (seriously, is that a dog or a chicken?)?
- ❏ Stopped talking to a friend after finding three soup cans in her garbage pail? (Never mind why I was snooping in

your garbage pail, *Carol!* The real issue is why you can't even take two seconds to peel the label off of a damn soup can and rinse it out for recycling!)

- ❑ Remembered to bring reusable bags to the grocery store?
- ❑ Brandished said reusable bags like trophies as you made your way to the checkout?
- ❑ Used a bag that reads "This Reusable Bag Makes Me Better Than You" . . .
- ❑ . . .and deep down kind of believe it?
- ❑ Reused a Ziploc bag?
- ❑ Reused a dog poop bag—No! Wait! Don't answer this. I don't want to know. I will judge you. We will *all* judge you.
- ❑ Ranted about any eco-related issue for more than fifteen minutes straight while the eyes of your unfortunate audience became ever more glassy and unfocused and the only other sound was the uncomfortable shuffling of feet as they tried to slowly back away from your saliva-strewn, invective-filled monologue?

RESULTS

If you scored seven points or more, you may just need to step away from the recycling bin, and put down the spray bottle of vinegar.

Take a deep breath, go hug your friends and beg for forgiveness. (Don't be surprised if they won't open the door unless you brandish a large bottle of wine and promise that your conversation won't include the words "sustainable," "green," "eco," or "carbon footprint.")

Once you guys have drunkenly hugged it out, get to work creating a daily mantra reminding yourself that, although it's wonderful to be passionate about environmentalism, it doesn't make you a better person. The mantra should be something simple yet direct like "Don't be a dick!"

But, I mean, that's just my suggestion. Feel free to make your own.

QUICK TIP

Ditch the paper towels and facial tissues. Tea towels and dishcloths work pretty much everywhere you'd use a paper towel, and you can employ newspaper for the truly gross messes. As for facial tissue, toilet paper works just as well at a fraction of the cost and without separate packaging. Why buy something twice?

Be gentle with yourself

The primary focus of this book is on our relationship with the natural world, and the many ways we can attempt to mitigate our negative environmental impact. There is a secondary relationship that I'm also hoping to address, however, and now seems as good a time as any.

The green movement has been incredibly successful at raising awareness of the eco-friendly changes we can make in our everyday lives, changes that many would argue we *need* to make in order to stop the earth from killing us all. But too often the rhetoric makes a subtle shift from empowering to guilt-inducing. I do understand the reasons behind this holier-than-thou proselytizing, but in my experience nothing is less conducive to creating positive habits than making people feel guilty.

Guilt breeds apathy, a feeling of being overwhelmed and inadequately prepared for the task at hand. We sit and stew, and the bad news and statistics and charts and graphs keep washing over our heads like waves until we find ourselves drowning in the sheer size of the problem. In the face of such a huge issue, it becomes easy to wonder what impact switching mascara brands will have.

As a result, we feel powerless. We feel guilty about not doing anything, but we also don't know what we *can* do, and our critical inner voice is given an entirely new topic to badger us about.

These days we not only feel bad if our homes aren't constantly magazine-ready, we also feel bad if we're not using "green" cleaners to get them there. There is immense societal pressure to be thin and beautiful and attractive, and now we must also try to meet these impossible standards while eating organic food prepared from scratch and wearing only natural mineral makeup.

This inner voice can be incredibly cruel. It is the embodiment of our deepest insecurities, and, if we spoke to our friends, our coworkers, or our partners the way we sometimes speak to ourselves, they wouldn't be in our lives for long.

It makes me sad to think that this whole "going green" movement has become just another thing to feel guilty about, one more checkmark on our ever-growing to-do list. It makes me sad because I think it has the potential to be far more than that. If done right it can foster a powerful sense of self-reliance, instead of a feeling of helplessness.

I remember the first time I realized I could make my own laundry detergent. I was reading the label of the super-expensive natural brand I usually bought, and decided to look up the ingredients. Slowly I began to realize that it was made up of little more than borax, washing soda, and essential oils. When referred to by their scientific names they all sounded pretty fancy, but they were ingredients I could purchase myself for a fraction of the price.

Staring at the computer screen, I remember thinking, "Wow. That is some real bs right there," and something clicked.

After I made my first batch of laundry detergent and realized how simple it was, and how easy, I felt incredibly proud. Embarrassingly proud, actually. It gave me a surprisingly strong feeling of autonomy and self-sufficiency when I realized that I didn't have to depend on giant corporations to provide products for me, I could create them myself.

I mean when was the last time you *made* something?

Choosing to live an eco-friendly, natural life also helps us let go of many of the unattainable standards we have for ourselves, because often they are fundamentally incompatible with environmentally friendly living.

Natural living, by its very definition, implies some measure of imperfection. It's not the immaculate house with perfectly pleated drapes and a couch no one has ever sat on. It's not clothing that's been perfectly dry-cleaned and starched. It's not a face sculpted by scalpels to look more symmetric.

Natural is a bit worn and lived-in. It is welcoming and comfortable like the crinkles around a person's eyes that hint at a lifetime of happiness. Natural is forgiving and warm, and it shouldn't be just another thing to feel bad about. If I had the power, I'd steer this whole eco-friendly boat away from the guilt and the one-upping and back to that warm space, back to that sense of feeling good by doing good.

So, while it's great that you are excited to dive head first into this whole eco-friendly thing, make sure you're friendly to yourself too. Be gentle in your self-talk, and don't spend your days chastising yourself for all the things you are not doing, instead of recognizing all that you are.

No one can implement change on a large scale all at once—and no one is expecting you to either. It's why I've tried to provide options instead of edicts. It's honestly OK if you don't want to wash your hair with vinegar (but if or when you do, I'll be here to show you how!).

Be kind to yourself. Be kind to your body, be kind to the life you have built for yourself and the things you have achieved. Be aware of that inner critic and that insidious negative voice.

Allow yourself to recognize the good you are doing, let each small success propel you forward, and while you are trying to nurture your relationship to good ol' Mother Earth, remember to nurture yourself too.

How living green can save your relationship

Have you ever noticed how *happy* hippies are with their beads and their tie dye and their guttural exclamations of, "Right on, *mannnnnn*"? Well, there's a reason for all those smiles and peace signs, and it goes well beyond those funny herbs they're smoking.

I wish to hypothesize that an eco-friendly lifestyle can actually make your relationship better. Typically, there are three main areas of conflict in a relationship: money, household chores, and sex. Sometimes it's just one that plagues a relationship, sometimes it's all three, but, more often than not, if one issue is left to fester long enough, it will spill over and cause a snowball effect, creating problems in the other two areas as well.

So what may have initially started as one person's overzealous use of credit cards on shopping binges soon turns into a house that is crammed and cluttered with all those useless purchases, and, lord knows, no sex is happening when you're stressed about money and sitting in a room full of crap, glaring at each other.

Now, before I delve into my theory, I'm going to say that I do not have a perfect relationship. If you remember my telling you that my husband used a trail of chocolate to lure me to our bedroom, where he then jumped out from behind the door wearing a stocking mask, I'll admit that taking the time to say that may seem a bit redundant.

I am mentioning it, however, because when you are talking about relationships it doesn't take much to feel as though you are veering into self-help territory, where an expert has the cure-all method for every issue that ever ailed your partnership, and look! It works! Because the expert has been married a million years and look how happy he or she looks in promotional photos!

But the mighty have a way of falling, don't they? And often, three years after spending hundreds of dollars on some expert's books and workshops, you'll find yourself reading about how she was cheating and he never loved her and, dang, it was a sham all along.

Well, you're not going to have to worry about that here. I will happily admit to all who care to hear it that my marriage has been a sham from the start. I'm pretty sure Adam is only with me for my vast fortune, and it's pretty obvious to anyone who knows us that I am just after his sweet dance moves. Ours is a marriage of attrition: we're just waiting around to see who cracks first.

Now that that disclaimer is out of the way and the flawless façade of my marriage is shot, I'll explain my hypothesis.

I think that if we apply the same eco-friendly ideas to our relationships that we do to other aspects of our lives, we can reduce stress, cut down on those big three sources of conflict, and bring back the joy we had at the beginning. Tall order—right?

Well let's start with reducing stress. Do you remember when you two first started dating? Everything was all giggles and rainbows, holding hands and movie nights. If things seemed so effortless and easy and *fun,* it's because they were! You didn't have to juggle two full-time jobs and a mortgage payment, and scrap over whose turn it was to change the oil in the car.

You hadn't yet discovered the horrible rollercoaster of bliss and rage that is coexisting under the same roof with someone who thinks it's funny to hide beer cans between the collected works of Atwood and Ondaatje on your bookshelf.

Much of the stress we experience in our day-to-day lives stems from our possessions—having enough money to buy them in the first place, then finding the time to organize them, repair them, replace them, and so on. We stress about working enough hours to have the means to afford the things we like, and then these things end up being just another source of unhappiness.

If you can somehow manage to apply the principle of reducing to take control of your possessions and de-clutter your home, however, the stress-savings might just spill over into your relationship. Use your hard-earned dollars to buy experiences—like mini-vacations or a babysitter for an evening—rather than more stuff. Use the time not spent organizing and tidying and cleaning, to spend with each other instead. It will feel so much nicer to gaze deeply into your partner's eyes and trade foot massages, than make strangling gestures behind his back as he stomps out of the room.

(And I mean, no, Adam and I haven't ever *actually* spent time staring into each other's eyes, or trading foot massages. But, I mean, we *could*. We have the *time* to, if we *wanted* to. OK?)

You can also consider reducing your commitments outside the home. Board meetings, work, team sports, secret parking-lot cheeseburger binges—these all eat away at the time you share with each other. It's hard to feel affectionate for someone you see for ten minutes when you wake up and five before you go to bed—especially when most of that time is spent coordinating the practical tasks in your life.

If you are some sort of Svengali, you could also try roping your partner into helping you with some of the green-cleaning methods mentioned in earlier chapters—not only will you be getting help with those nitty-gritty chores, but you might even gain some shared interests too. (The experts say that having shared goals and interests is, apparently, good for a relationship or something? All I know is that up until a few years ago, the closest Adam and I got to "shared interests" was sitting in silence watching Gus lick himself. These days he helps me grate soap, hang diapers on the clothesline, and brainstorm different ways to reduce our stuff and simplify our lives. Winning!)

I find that things are more likely to get done, and get done with the least amount of rage, when we're working alongside each other, instead of me having a fit barking orders and issuing edicts. Weird.

It's not like we're curing cancer or anything, but those experts must be on to something because there is something inexplicably delicious about working alongside each other toward a common goal. Obviously, scrubbing your bathtub with baking soda isn't going to save your relationship, but often just taking some time to examine what we are doing, and why, can really help.

It's easy for our lives to become as cluttered as our cupboards, but getting rid of all the superfluous junk and replacing it with meaningful experiences and full bank accounts will have an overall effect of reducing your overall stress levels too. Remember those big three issues we fight about: sex, money, household chores.

Reducing your purchases and your possessions will help reduce arguments about money. Reducing your Honey-Do list and taking the time to tackle chores together cuts down on resentment as well as those naggings jobs that never seem to get done. Best of all, once you've sorted out all that friction over money and chores, that newfound harmony can't help but spill over into the third area too.

Those hippies. They're on to something, mannnnnnn.

GOOD GIFTS

If popular advertising is to be believed, the pinnacle of a romantic relationship is achieved when a white male buys a white female a piece of jewelry that costs several hundreds (or thousands) of dollars. By doing so, he fulfills his culturally appropriate role, and she gets to display this bauble for the world to admire. Everyone involved is sufficiently convinced of his good financial standing as well as his fealty to said female, and everyone's happy!

Or ARE they?! (Dun dun dun dunnnnnn!)

Giving jewelry as a token of your love is a tradition that goes back centuries, built on beliefs we all seem to accept with little or no question about the tradition itself. But you know what? I think it's about time we did. Guys, let's blow this thing wide open!

Without getting too deep into the *meaning* of it all, I'd like to quickly rip apart a few of the assumptions implicit in nearly every jewelry store advertisement out there:

1. **Not all couples are male-female**. I have yet to see one same-sex, transgender, or other "unconventional" relationship represented by a major jewelry store.
2. **Not all couples are white**. If you looked at most advertisements for diamond rings or gold pendants, you would assume that people of color simply don't buy jewelry.
3. **Jewelry ≠ love. Love ≠ jewelry.** The way these two things have become slimily intertwined makes my skin itch. Does it really take little more than a shiny trinket to elicit a kiss, or even a promise to spend a lifetime together? Conversely, is your commitment any less sincere if you don't have, or don't *want*, the bling to back it up?
4. **Precious gems and metals leave a horrific trail of pollution and human rights abuses.** Not much more needs to be said about this one without getting into some seriously depressing territory, but we cannot discuss jewelry without acknowledging that many people pay a steep price in order to mine, produce, and export precious metals and all those shiny little rocks we coyly call "a girl's best friend."

I swear I'm not a total jerk about this particular subject. I do own jewelry, and much of it holds great meaning to me. If you get engaged, flash me that rock and I will ooh and aah over it, and nowhere in my sincere congratulations will you hear one word about human rights abuses.

I'm truly not trying to trash your life or make you feel horrible for wanting pretty earrings. I am, however, trying to examine, and then expand, the definition of what a "good gift" is, so that we as a society and as individuals can begin to reach beyond this category for the benefit of all involved.

First of all, let's realize that we are being encouraged to want expensive jewelry just as we are encouraged to buy expensive cleaners and fancy face creams that smell nice but don't really do anything. Diamonds are one of the most common gemstones on earth, and were a relatively unpopular choice for engagement rings prior to 1930. Their current popularity is due to a carefully engineered decades-long marketing campaign. Similarly, it has been drilled into us that a romantic occasion is nothing without the little blue box to back it up.

It's fine if you like jewelry, it's fine if you choose to give it and receive it, but if we don't question, examine, and look for other options, we're not making a choice, we're just blindly following what popular societal norms tell us to do. And how romantic is that?

The love stories that capture our attention and live on indefinitely are the unconventional ones, the ones that defy logic and chance and thrive in difficult times. The love stories we love to hear all have something that sets them apart from the masses. So be different! Set yourself apart. Look beyond the diamond, and the jewelry store, and the little blue box.

Give a gift that speaks to something other than modern-day slavery and the mining of natural resources. Give something intangible and unexpected—something you don't have to worry about, store, insure, and clean.

Here are some alternate ideas for gifts that will run you about the same price as a shiny bracelet:

- A weekend getaway at a B&B
- An adventure—zip lining, white-water rafting, a kayak tour, or a horseback ride
- A deep tissue massage (I think I just uttered an involuntary moan when I typed that. I'm going to suggest it again just in case anyone didn't catch it the first time around)
- A DEEP TISSUE MASSAGE
- Something your loved one really needs but wouldn't necessarily shell out for himself—like a good quality knife set
- Pay for and coordinate a surprise visit from a much beloved and missed friend or relative
- Go old-school and make a coupon book for chores, home pampering, or tasks you know they hate
- Glamour photos. GLAMOUR. PHOTOS. Imagine the possibilities!
- Etc., and so on

- OK think of a few of your own now
- Seriously, I can't do all your work for you

The idea of giving experiences rather than tangible gifts works for all gifts, incidentally, not just romantic ones.

Doing this as a matter of habit will make for a dresser less cluttered and a life rich with memories—like that time your best friend got you a massage for your birthday and the masseuse paid a little too much attention to your glutes, which was kind of "Ew," but also kind of "Hey! Still got it!"

MAKE IT

Personal lubricant

Clearly, the last thing you want to be thinking about when you're getting down and dirty is whether or not your lube is chock-full of phthalates, parabens, or other very non-sexy stuff. Also, having a mid-coitus freak-out over the ingredients of your lubricant can be a real turn off, I hear. Allegedly.

Friends, if you are going to choose just ONE thing to be picky about, this should be it.

Making your own lubricant is not only earth- and private-parts friendly, but also a built-in solution for anyone too shy to set foot in a sex store or march up to the counter of the supermarket brandishing a big bottle of KY.

Luckily, this is an easy-peasy change to make and requires very little effort.

As a general rule, if the oil is safe to eat, you can go ahead and get jiggy with it. Unrefined coconut oil, olive oil, and avocado oil are all great options to replace store-bought lubricants; they offer all the same benefits without any of the nasty additives.

Transfer some of your oil of choice to a jar or squeeze top container, and keep it in your bedside drawer. That's a universal thing, right? In my world, bedside drawer = sex drawer, so snoop at your own risk, y'all.

Now, although this tip couldn't be any easier, there are some things to be aware of. Like you might want to put down a towel because some oils can stain sheets. But, most importantly, please note that while these natural options are earth-friendly they are NOT latex-friendly.

I'm going to repeat myself, because I really don't want to see you guys a year from now toting around a whole bunch of accidental hippie babies: DO NOT USE OIL-BASED LUBRICANTS WITH LATEX CONDOMS. The two simply don't mix.

If you want the best of both worlds—a natural lubricant AND safe-sex peace of mind—gather up your courage and take a trip down to your local sex-positive romance shop (or for the more timid amongst us, online) to find a water-based lubricant.

It will be safe for condoms and gentle on your bits and pieces too.

Massage oil

Back massages are one of my favorite things in the entire world. If I was a lady of indiscriminate means and immense wealth I would employ a full-time masseuse to give me back massages approximately eighteen times a day, every day.

These wouldn't be namby-pamby relaxation massages either—I want the type of massage where they jam their elbow into your spine and find knots you never even knew existed. I think I might be drooling a little bit just thinking about it.

Sadly, I am not immensely wealthy and in my house back massages do not happen eighteen times a day. Instead, they happen whenever I can manage to beg, bribe, or cajole Adam into servitude, whereupon I receive a few blissful moments of decent massage before the whole thing devolves into a haphazard sort of groping.

Let's forget all that, however, and pretend that you have a great and desperate need for massage oil, so much so that you need to make it yourself because it's getting too pricey to pay retail at your current rate of use.

Lo! A recipe!

INGREDIENTS

1 cup almond, jojoba, or (untoasted) sesame oil—or a blend of all three

10–15 drops of the essential oils of your choice

Pour the oils into a jar and mix well. For a nice, warm oil massage, set the jar in a bowl of hot water for a few minutes.

My favorite essential-oil combinations include sweet orange with vanilla, lavender with eucalyptus, and bergamot all by its lovely self.

QUICK TIP

Physical touch is essential for the physical, psychological, and emotional health of human beings. Massage in particular has been shown to help fight depression, decrease blood pressure and cortisol (stress) levels, and boost white blood cell counts. It's safe, all-natural, and even gluten-free!

You know, just in case you ever needed a *reason* to get a massage.

CHAPTER 7

Health & Wellness

APPLE CIDER VINEGAR CURES EVERYTHING

A film came out in 2002 entitled *My Big Fat Greek Wedding*. In the film, the main character's father is an adorable old Greek man named Gus Portokalos. I remember watching the film as a tender nineteen-year-old and falling head over heels in love with the guy—and not just because his name was Gus. He was just this sweet, passionate, hilarious man whom I ached to hug, or high five, or put in my pocket and take home with me so that he could dispense his peculiar brand of Greek wisdom whenever my course in life faltered (which at nineteen was *often*).

I think that part of the affection I felt for dear old Gus was due to his unnatural affinity for Windex—it was his go-to, cure-all solution for absolutely everything that ailed a person, from poison ivy to psoriasis. As I became more and more ~~crazy~~ environmentally conscious throughout the years, Adam has often teased that apple cider vinegar is my Windex, and guys, he's kind of right.

He doesn't even bother complaining to me about physical ailments anymore, because my answer is invariably "ACV!"—just when you thought that living with me couldn't get any more insufferable with the baking soda and the recycling, here we are!

Here is just a taste of the many, many (many) things you can cure with this wunderkind potion (I've included page numbers to find recipes where relevant):

- Facial toner (page 60)
- Hair conditioner (page 54)
- Sore throat soother (dilute a few tablespoons in a large glass of water and drink)
- Flea repellent (page 230)
- Heartburn cure (drink 1–2 tablespoons diluted in a large glass of water)
- Sunburn reliever—add 1 cup to a bath and soak
- Toe-fungus eliminator (swipe with a cotton ball soaked in ACV)

  Bug bite soother (swipe with a cotton ball soaked in ACV)
- Digestion aid (drink 1 tbsp. diluted in a cup of warm water before every meal)

- Itchy-skin calmer (add ½ cup to a warm bath)
- And it's even fantastic on kale chips. BOOM!

ALTERNATIVE THERAPIES

I recently read an article about the placebo effect, stating that the cure rates of placebos range from 15 to 72 percent.[15] For someone like me who believes in a lot of ridiculous nonsense, this was like winning the lottery. I sent the article to all my friends with the subject line, "I'm not crazy! YOU'RE crazy!"

If you're unfamiliar with the term, the placebo effect refers to a fascinating phenomenon whereby a placebo (or fake medicine, often something like a sugar pill or saline injection) can improve a patient's condition just as effectively as an actual medication or medical intervention—simply because the patient *believes* it will. Often, the more faith the patient puts in the fake treatment, the more effective it is found to be.

The placebo effect has been demonstrated countless times with varying degrees of success, typically by conducting a double-blind study in which one half of a group receives real treatment, and the other half receives a placebo, without knowing which is which. What this study, the one I gleefully forwarded to everyone I knew, showed was that, interestingly enough, sometimes up to 72 percent of a control group that received placebo pills experienced the same positive effects as the test group who received actual medicine.

What does all this scientific jibber-jabber mean? It means that, for a great number of us, the medicine we are paying for, diligently taking, and even sometimes suffering side effects from may not have a whole lot to do with the positive effects we are experiencing. In many cases, popping a Tic-Tac might have had the same effect, because, guys, we are literally curing ourselves with our MINDS!

This is bad news for multi-million-dollar pharmaceutical companies, but great news for the manufacturers of sugar-pills—and for crazy hippies.

I often reference the placebo effect when explaining my choice to explore alternative therapies wherever possible. I look at it this way: Given the choice between an acupuncture treatment or a pill that has eleventy-seven side effects (many of which seem just as bad, if not worse, than the condition I'm trying to cure), I'm trying the acupuncture first, every time.

I'm not a doctor or a scientist, and I have no idea if sticking needles in my face truly has any effect, but it doesn't cause any harm either, and I now have hard data to back up the fact that if I believe in this nonsense hard enough, it just might work.

(Obviously this approach is more suited to treating minor ailments than serious illnesses, and even being solidly in the pro-alternative therapies camp as I am, I would still advise deferring to a doctor's opinion on all serious health matters.)

Our minds are incredibly powerful, and we cannot underestimate the role they play in determining our moods, our performance, and, yes, even our physical health. Even if you don't approve of this scattershot approach to minor healthcare issues, it is worth investigating alternative therapies if only to give yourself some perspective on how powerful the mind can be when tasked to heal the body.

I don't mean this in a crazy "I can mend bones with my rainbow thoughts!" type of way, but more that it's OK to acknowledge that your mood affects your stress levels, which cause chemicals like cortisol and norepinephrine to be released into your bloodstream, which in turn affect your heart rate and breathing, which *then* affect how much blood and oxygen are being shunted to every vital organ in your entire body, and—gosh, this is all sounding not quite so crazy all of a sudden!

Be a crazy hippie. Just a little bit. Try ditching the pills and get some needles stuck in your face instead—see what happens.

QUICK TIP

White vinegar does double duty in the wash as a fabric softener and an odor eliminator, especially if you're washing cloth diapers. Just add some to the fabric softener dispenser of your washing machine, or fill one of those fabric softener balls if you have one. The vinegar softens clothing without coating fibers in chemical goo or leaving harsh scents behind.

HOW (AND WHY) TO STICK A SMALL CERAMIC TEAPOT UP YOUR NOSE

It's called a neti pot, and it changed my life.

It originated in the ancient Hindu practice of Ayurveda and was originally thought to have a role in cleansing the spirit as well as the sinuses, but I think my spirit is doing pretty well, so I mostly just use it when I'm stuffed up and don't want to rip through a million wads of toilet paper.

Everyone hates the burn of a nose blown too many times, and the environmental impact of all that tissue can't be ignored. This is an easy way to avoid both of those inconvenient truths (see what I did there?).

First find yourself a neti pot. This is one of the rare instances when I encourage you to buy new, because *gross*.

Neti pots are often sold at larger drug stores or pharmacies, and definitely at health food stores. They typically come in plastic or ceramic—indulge my hatred of all things plastic and choose the latter.

Basically, what you are doing with this little teapot is putting it inside one nostril, pouring a saline solution into your sinuses and letting it flow like a stream out the other nostril—taking with it any mucus, dust, or irritants it has picked up along the way.

Neti pots often come with pre-measured pouches of solution that you just add water to, but if yours didn't it is easy to create your own. Never use a neti pot with just plain water, as doing so can irritate your delicate nasal membranes.

To create your saline solution, I like to boil and cool the water I'll be using, to make sure it's sterile. Once it's lukewarm, mix 1 cup of water and ¼ teaspoon of finely ground sea salt.

Make sure to stir the water thoroughly until the salt is dissolved, then put the spout of the neti pot in one nostril. Tip your head to the side at roughly a 45-degree angle with your chin away from your chest, begin breathing through your mouth, and then pour!

If you have the technique down pat the water will flow effortlessly in one nostril and out the next, and your husband will look at you like you have lost your damn mind.

It sometimes takes a few tries to get the hang of it, so if you know a neti-pot user, bribe her to come over and show you the ropes. If, however, you are the first one in your circle to decide that snorting saltwater sounds like a good time, watching a few YouTube videos on the subject can really help you get the technique right.

After flushing one side, blow your nose to get rid of any excess water. (But *never* plug one nostril while doing so, as you run the risk of forcing water back into your sinuses. Always blow with both nostrils open). Then repeat the process on the other side.

I swear, nothing works better than a good neti pot session when I'm feeling congested. It's fantastic for those who have sinus problems, and I never end up looking like Rudolph from too much nose-blowing either.

MAKE IT

Magic tea for cold and flu season

After having a good old time with the neti pot, you might want to brew up some of this tea as a cure-all for aches and pains, sore throats, and those days when you just want to crawl under the covers and die a slow, dramatic death.

This is particularly effective for the phenomenon known in our house as the "Man Cold." It goes like this:

When I get sick: I try to stay in bed as much as possible, and after much cajoling, begging, bribing, threatening, etc., I am sometimes successful in convincing Adam to rub my aching back. My illnesses usually last one or two days, during which time I am still doing all the writing, chores, and baby-tending that I usually do, albeit at a slower pace and with 100 percent more long-suffering sighs. (I figure I'm entitled to that much.)

When Adam gets sick: End. Of. The. World. Seriously, did you know that a cold could kill you? Because, guys, he is dying. DYING! How do I know this? I know this because he helpfully tells me at least three times an hour. And you know what? I'm actually starting to believe him. What other reason could there be for all those horrendous moans and groans, and the way he winces as he shifts the weight of his poor decrepit body into a better position to watch 12 consecutive hours of *Storage Wars?*

All other activities are suspended for the duration of the Man Cold—including mine, because nursing him back to health is now my full-time job. I am a good wife, so I offer the sort of sustenance that befits an ailing body: hot teas, nourishing soups, and such. He lets these go cold in favor of nestling into an ever-growing pile of popsicle wrappers—and not even the somewhat less-horrible "real fruit" kind where you can trick yourself into thinking you're eating something healthy, but the old-school, pure sugar, neon kind.

Anytime I balk at fulfilling his increasingly extravagant demands I am reminded in a pitiful tone of our wedding vows where I promised to love him "'...in sickness and in health/Till death do us part'.... And, Madeleine, I think I might *actually* be dying" (dramatic wheeze).

Why is this my life?

Clearly, these sorts of shenanigans are completely unsustainable. Thus, it is in my best interest to cure the Man Cold as soon as it begins. Enter the Magic Tea.

I think it works just as well as the store-bought cold and flu teas without all the weird side effects or unpronounceable ingredients, plus you get to look like a bit of a witch doctor while you're making it.

Whenever I am able to wrench the popsicles from his hand and force a cup or two down Adam's throat, I've always had favorable results, and actually this is one of the few natural remedies that he will go out of his way to ask for. You could call it Adam Approved.

MADELEINE'S MAGIC TEA

Bring 4 cups of water to boil, and add:

½ lemon, thinly sliced

1 tablespoon honey

1 clove of garlic, thinly sliced

2 teaspoons coarsely grated ginger

A pinch of cayenne pepper

Reduce heat and simmer your concoction for 5–10 minutes.

Each ingredient in this magic tea plays a role in healing, as well as easing symptoms of colds and flu: Ginger is thought to aid in digestion and act as an anti-inflammatory for sore muscles, garlic is a powerful antifungal, lemon juice cleanses and purifies, honey coats and soothes sore throats, and cayenne pepper helps move mucus and ease headache pains.

For best results, drink 2–3 times a day.

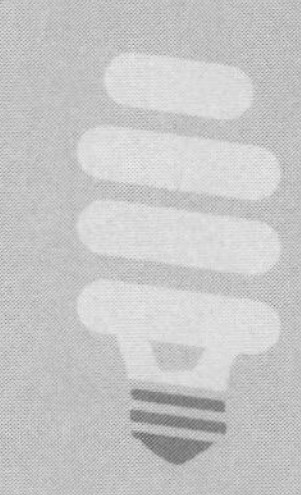

QUICK TIP

If you have a persistent cough, rub a few drops of eucalyptus oil onto the soles of your feet. I have no idea why this works, but it does. Hippie magic!

Epsom salt aromatherapy bath

When all your muscles ache from head to toe, whether from a nasty cold or just a particularly intense stripperobics class (the pole can be a cruel mistress), an Epsom salt bath is one of the best things you can do to ease the pain—second only to an actual massage by an actual masseuse who actually *massages* you instead of just giving a few haphazard squeezes in and around your neck area before wandering around to your boobs, A*dam*.

Epsom salts are also known as magnesium sulfate, and magnesium is one of the body's most essential minerals. I like to consider myself a bit of an expert in this field because my parents were kind enough to gift me with a rare chronic kidney disease called Gitelman Syndrome, which causes extreme electrolyte deficiencies.

Let me tell you, nothing makes you more aware of how important something is than when it's missing. This is true of big things like love, and small things like candy. Magnesium, I think, ranks somewhere in the middle.

This mineral is tasked with an astonishing myriad of functions, and if you are magnesium deficient you get to experience delights like depression, anxiety, muscle tightness, tremors, poor memory, and fatigue. I am telling you all this because, even though you might not be lucky enough to have such a rare kidney disease with such a glamorous name, it's estimated that roughly 75 percent of North Americans are magnesium deficient.[16] So there you were feeling sorry for me, and now we find out that you ARE me! Well, three-quarters of you, anyway.

Just a bunch of depressed, anxious, tight-muscled, tremor-y, forgetful little stress-balls. No wonder we need a hot bath.

Epsom salts can be found at many grocery stories, pharmacies, and drugstores, and they offer a great way to absorb the good stuff, as well as offering a bit of mental relaxation as well.

These aren't dainty little bath salts you'll be adding by the teaspoon, however. You'll need one to two cups per bath, so buy the big jug when you can. Sometimes you can buy Epsom salts in bulk, which is also quite convenient.

To make your aromatherapy bath, you'll need the following:

- An hour of peace and quiet (for those of you rolling your eyes because you have children, smart phones, busy lives, or all three, twenty minutes will suffice)
- A mixing bowl
- 1–2 cups of unscented Epsom salts
- 10–15 drops of your favorite essential oil

For an idea of which essential oil to use, here's a quick list of the therapeutic properties imbued by a few of the most popular:

- **Chamomile**: Soothing. Combats anxiety, irritability and stress.
- **Grapefruit**: Energizing, refreshing. Fights lethargy.
- **Jasmine**: Aphrodisiac. Helps with tension and apathy.

- **Lavender**: Calming and balancing. Helps with depression, anxiety, and fear. (My personal favorite.) (Lavender, that is. Not fear.)
- **Orange**: Sedative properties. Eases anxiety and insomnia.
- **Patchouli**: Calming, anti-inflammatory. Helps fight anxiety and can help to ground you.
- **Peppermint**: Energizing and stimulating. Refreshes and awakens.
- **Sandalwood**: Soothing, sedative. Helps with apprehension and shyness.

This little cheat sheet spells out what each essential oil is traditionally used for, but smell is an incredibly personal sense that can evoke intense memories and strong associations. If the scent of lavender reminds you of your grandmother, who—though a lovely woman—was also a particularly feisty and acerbic individual, it probably won't have the calming benefits for which it is often prescribed.

Use the chart as a rough guide to choose scents that are meant to calm, soothe, and balance, but use your own senses to find an essential oil that inspires you to give a great big exhale. That's the one for you.

When you've picked the right oil, add 1–2 cups of Epsom salts to a large mixing bowl along with 10–15 drops of your essential oils, and give it a good stir. Let everything set for a few moments while you run your bath, then pour the whole thing in and stir to dissolve completely.

Your bath will be salty, so now is not the time to wash your hair, shave your legs, or do any other cleansing ritual. Just lie back and relax, take deep breaths, and even do some *om*-chanting, if you're into that sort of thing. Beeswax candles are a nice touch.

Make sure to drink lots of water during and after your bath to help relax those muscles, and if you'd like to extend the relaxation even further, consider an aprės-bath coconut oil massage (more info on page 48).

CHAPTER 8

Baby

WELCOMING YOUR ADORABLE LITTLE WASTE MACHINE

As I write this, I am four months pregnant and have just completed my first foray into prenatal consumption; I bought ginormous, stretchy maternity leggings. The waistband pulls up to just under my armpits and they are simultaneously the least sexy and most indescribably *awesome* piece of clothing I have ever owned.

The purchase of these gargantuan leggings is a big deal for two reasons (three if you include the fact that their inclusion in my wardrobe means that I am really and truly unavoidably actually *pregnant*):

1. I don't often buy clothing, especially items I can see myself wearing for only six months, tops.

2. It represents the reversal of one of my strongest pre-pregnancy ideals. You see, I used to mock maternity wear in all its incarnations, and was smugly confident that I could breeze through my nine-month gestation wearing all the same clothing I already owned.

(If you're wondering how I convinced myself that this would be possible while my waist expanded to more than double its normal size, the answer is apparently a combination of stupidity and an extremely poor grasp of physics.)

But, physics be damned, this was my plan. I stubbornly maintained that I wouldn't need to buy anything new—it was obvious to me that every pregnant lady before me was a dimwitted automaton, mindlessly gravitating toward maternity-marketing like a moth to a flame. "Not me!" I vowed. "I'm different!"

(That sound you hear is every woman who has tried to squeeze her four-month-pregnant self into skinny jeans having a good laugh at my *ignorance*.)

Needless to say, I was wrong. When my pre-pregnancy clothing started to leave deep red indentations on my expanding belly I finally, and reluctantly, recanted. I renounced my maternity-clothing-hating ways, and today in the dressing room of a maternity store I pulled a giant band of soft fabric over my midsection and found myself at a complete loss for words.

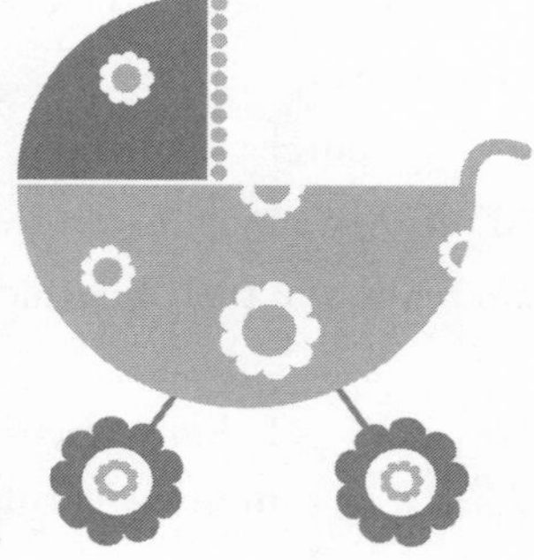

I was completely enamored of this new world, dreamily swaying back and forth within the roomy confines of my big, stretchy, forever home. I am not ashamed to say that I am wearing those leggings right now, and I never, ever want to take them off.

This long-winded preamble is to let you know, fellow parent or pregnant person, *I get it*. Having children does inevitably involve the acquisition of stuff—even if you initially vow otherwise.

Kids need things, sometimes even before they arrive in this world, and although I am relishing these last few childless months as the only time when I will have all the answers to parenting, I will not be recommending that your babe play with exclusively organic wood toys or wear exclusively pesticide-free hemp onesies.

On the other hand, I think we can all agree that our nation has gone thoroughly, excessively baby-crazy. When the average three-year-old has a more extensive clothing and accessory collection than a thirty-year-old woman, we as a society have some serious 'splainin to do.

It can be hard to remain steadfastly committed to a simple, eco-conscious lifestyle when baby's on the way. From the moment you share the good news, well-meaning friends and family seem to converge en masse, proffering gifts of tiny adorable outfits and brightly colored play centers.

Friends with older children will suddenly appear on your doorstep with a minivan crammed to the rooftop with noise-making, battery-needing toys, cheerfully announcing that they just cleaned out their children's playroom and thought you could use a few things.

Um…thanks?

Please believe me when I say that however bad you think the gift-giving is pre-baby, it will only get worse. Holidays will come and go, birthdays will pass, and if you're not careful, your dreams of a minimalist playroom will soon be buried beneath a mountain of junk.

This chapter will give you a few helpful ideas about how to acquire all the stuff you genuinely do need in an eco- (and wallet-) friendly manner, as well as tips for stemming the tide of unnecessary stuff from friends and family.

Hitch up your maternity leggings, friends, and let's begin!

WHY CRAIGSLIST SHOULD BE YOUR BABY'S MIDDLE NAME

You're pregnant! Or the adoption has gone through! Or you found a surrogate! Whichever way you have chosen to grow your family, congratulations are in order—you are in for a wild and beautiful ride, my friend.

Feel free to take a few months to let this life-changing news settle in. Enjoy the butterflies of nervousness, and savor every little thrill of anticipation. Then, after the savoring and the butterflies, we need to get down to business, because this here process I'm going to tell you about may take some time.

You remember how I ranted on and on about the benefits of buying secondhand in Chapter 1? Well, this is sort of the same idea. Except that, rather than choosing to buy secondhand as a method of evaluating how a product stands up to normal use, you're doing the exact opposite. You're buying items precisely because they haven't been used much, and aren't likely to be.

Barring a few items like bibs or mattresses, baby items typically undergo extremely light use—especially clothing. You can pretty much guarantee that the onesie you're eyeing has been worn for three months or less, and is probably in absolutely perfect condition. This is why buying secondhand baby stuff is probably the single smartest thing you can do as a parent.

There's also the fact that, until your munchkin is here in your arms, you will have no idea if that $200 swing will end up being your secret weapon in getting your little angel to sleep, or if she'll loathe it so much that its only useful feature is the white-noise machine, which does an admirable job of muffling your exhausted sobs.

(If it's the latter, I've been there. I feel for you, and I so wish that I could send a hug and a coffee your way. I promise you, though, that you will feel a teensy bit better about this whole situation if you found that $200 swing used on Craigslist and only paid fifty dollars for it. Even sleep-deprived zombies love a good deal—right?)

Swings, gliders, baby carriers, strollers, and baby clothing are usually fairly easy to come by secondhand. Hit up Craigslist, your local secondhand stores, consignment stores, and even Facebook for a great deal. (Many cities have a local Facebook Baby Buy & Sell group, and mine was absolutely invaluable in stocking up for the arrival of little Olive.)

Instead of getting sleepers for ten to fifteen dollars each, I often found them for as little as a dollar, and I had an incredible selection to choose from. I also liked knowing that, as I was building Olive's wardrobe, I was also saving money and helping another mom free up some space in her closet.

It can also be a good idea to call around to local mom-and-baby meet-up groups. Some host free clothing exchanges every six weeks or so, which tends to be just the right amount of time to reevaluate your little one's wardrobe and donate items that don't fit, as well as stock up on items you don't have. If there isn't a local group that offers this, just pretend that you thought of the idea yourself and offer to host one—you will receive a million Mom Genius accolades! (You're welcome).

A word of warning, however, when you're finding baby clothes for a dollar—or free!—it can be tough to resist the temptation to go crazy. Just because you're paying 90 percent less doesn't mean you should purchase 90 percent more. Remember that your baby is probably going to keep wearing your favorite four or five outfits over and over again, while everything else clutters up his drawers until you realize he has outgrown them. Make a reasonable list and stick to it.

Beyond clothing lies the strange and bewildering world of baby gear, and for every weird unitasking "must-have" item there are a hundred lists supporting its purchase. As a first-time or expectant parent you easily get pressured into purchasing these things for fear of being unprepared. But let me reassure you/terrify you by saying that there is absolutely no way that you will *ever* be prepared.

Seriously, unless you have been a full-time slave to a tiny screaming dictator before, nothing can ever prepare you for having a child, and no number of white noise machines or fancy baby baths will do anything to change that.

It's also an unfortunate reality that one person's absolutely essential die-if-you-don't-have-it baby item is another person's useless, trip-over-it-every-time-I-go-to-the-basement-where-it-sits-gathering-dust item. Our solution to this was to calmly acknowledge that stores would continue to exist after the birth of our child, and rather than buy everything before having Olive, we bought only the basics, (like, *really* basic: think a place to sleep, clothing, diapers, blankets), and if we found that we needed something in the course of taking care of our little one, we would purchase it then.

This really helped deal with my instinct to BUY EVERYTHING! JUST IN CASE!

In case of what, you ask? IRRELEVANT!

Luckily, one of us wasn't under the influence of crazy pregnancy hormones, and we managed to follow through on our plan—buying basic stuff secondhand and not buying anything else at all.

The result of this backwards provisioning is that we never had the following "must-haves":

- Baby monitor. She slept in a crib in our room for the first six months, and our house was so small that we could hear her from pretty much any room.
- Bassinette (see above)
- Baby bath. We used the sink, and then, as she outgrew that, we either bathed with her, or popped her in the big tub.
- Stroller. I know. *I know.* It seems crazy but, as I write this, Olive is almost six months old, we still don't own one, and there's only been a handful of times that I've wished we did. She was born in the winter when we knew there'd be too much snow to get much use out of a stroller anyway, so we bought a secondhand ErgoBaby carrier instead, and it's worked really well for us.

This list will look different for everyone, and the goal is not to exactly replicate our experience, nor to deprive yourself of things you truly need—raising an infant is hard enough without being an enviro-martyr to boot. But I will say that, by not having these things in the first place, we didn't know what we were missing.

If we truly *did* miss something, if we truly felt we couldn't live without it any longer, we were then able to purchase it and feel good about knowing that it was really needed.

My only caveat to this tip is to please use your discretion when buying secondhand gear like cribs, highchairs, playpens, or car seats. Ensure that the item is within the expiry date (where applicable), hasn't been included in any recall, and is in safe working condition.

Most states have their own laws about secondhand car seat sales, so check to see what's legal in your state or province, and, if you do choose to buy one secondhand, I'd recommend that you buy only from a friend or family member you trust to swear that it hasn't been in an accident.

Happy hunting!

TOYS, TOYS, TOYS

When your child is a newborn, you will be inundated with blankets and sleepers and dozens of baby shoes that are as impractical as they are adorable.

Once your child becomes more than a passive little lump, however, the toys start creeping in. An exersaucer here, an activity gym there, rattling toys and stroller toys and teething toys and toys to build fine motor skills and—mon dieu! Didn't you use to have a living room floor somewhere?

The key here is to set some limits for yourself—and for well-intentioned friends and relatives—in order to reduce the sheer volume of toys streaming into your home. The goal, as always, is quality over quantity. A handful of well-made, well-designed toys that your child loves to play with will trump a playroom full of junk any day. If your child has so many toys that he can find only half of them, the other half does little more than contribute to the clutter in your home, and your soaring stress/rage levels too.

What kind of limits you set is entirely up to you. You are the parent! Enforcing arbitrary laws will soon be your main job in life, so you may as well start now. The rules might be a polite request that your child receive secondhand toys only, or even a request for no toys at all, but I chose to take the sanctimonious route and declare a wholesale ban on any and all plastic toys. Period.

The reasons for this were many and varied, ranging from my hatred of the toxic nature of plastic playthings, all the way to their cheap quality, but it also had the wonderful side effect of disqualifying approximately 90 percent of toy purchases.

By eliminating toys made of plastic, I killed three birds with one stone: I got to tackle the insane amount of pollution created in its manufacture, production, and disposal; I reduced the number of toys cluttering our home; and I also got to come off like a sanctimonious, holier-than-thou hippie mom.

Success!

Sometimes the best toys are also the most simple—and often they aren't even toys at all. Pretty much the greatest thing you can give to a small child is a giant cardboard box—this simple object can, over the course of days or weeks, become a rocket-ship, a race-car, or a dollhouse—pretty much anything their little minds can dream up.

Pots and pans are enticingly loud and unbreakable, funnels and measuring cups make great bath toys, sheets and couch cushions make incredible forts, and, as an added bonus, while your child is happily unpacking your kitchen cupboards, deafening those around her and demolishing your pristine living room, she is learning a wholesome lesson in imagination and creative play.

(Meanwhile, you are also learning a lesson, and that lesson is called "How to Release Your Whiteknuckled Grasp on the Tidily Ordered World You Used to Know and Love.")

As for store-bought toys, fair-trade playthings made of wood, cloth, and other natural materials are tougher to find and also usually more expensive, but I choose to don my rose-colored glasses and look at this as a pro rather than a con. One of the reasons we settled on the no-plastic rule in the first place was that it meant we had to put some thought into our purchases, and both the price and availability of wood toys meant we could usually buy only one toy rather than, say, five.

When a wooden toy breaks it can be repaired. When the finish begins to get dull it can be sanded and repainted. And when your child chews on it—because babies, like tiny rabid wolf-children, chew on *everything*—you won't be worried about the toxic chemicals that may have been involved in their manufacture.

Plastic toys are part of that insidious buy-break-replace cycle we talked about earlier, and, even worse, advertisers market these toys directly to children too young to know better. Billions of dollars every year are spent trying to coerce your three-year-old into pestering you for the newest mass-manufactured must-have. The effect of this advertising on impressionable young minds concerns me almost as much as the effect of all these disposable toys on the world we leave them. Plastic is brittle and unforgiving, it off-gasses toxic chemicals, it breaks and wears down and fades. Plastic toys will sit inert in landfills for hundreds of thousands of years after your child has lost interest in them.

I know that all this can be challenging (and disheartening) to explain to a child who is desperate for the latest trendy toy of the season, but part of our role as parents is to be the bigger jerk, the one who says *no* for the greater good.

Even more important is to not pass up the chance to explain *why*, to impart a sense of stewardship and responsibility for this world we live in. I desperately want my daughter to grow up with an understanding about what it means to live in a sustainable way, why it's important to buy things that are well-constructed and fairly made, and what it means to consider the impact of your actions on those around you, as well as on the world we live in.

I want that so badly that I don't care if I come across as crazy.

Our children learn from us, and they learn from our actions and the way we make our choices as much—if not more so—than the lessons we take the time to explicitly teach.

It would feel disingenuous to teach Olive about recycling and reducing energy use while at the same time endorsing the incredibly wasteful trend of consumption and disposal so prevalent in our culture.

In the days and weeks after Olive was born, I would sit for hours with her in my arms, staring at her tiny eyelashes and tightly balled fists. Along with an overwhelming desire to protect her at all costs, I began to feel an intense need to leave this world a better place than I found it, for her sake. Many people choose to have children so that a part of them will continue to live on, long after they cease to—and in those wee morning hours, I began to ask myself what that life would look like.

The best part of taking the initiative to create a sustainable life for yourself is that you are giving your children a head start on doing the same.

When they have outgrown wooden rattles and brightly colored stacking blocks, when their first tentative steps have turned into a full-tilt run toward independence, and when you have folded up the last of the baby clothes and that tiny lump of an infant can walk and talk and pee on the potty like a *real human person,* you will know that he won't have left a trail of plastic trash in his wake.

He'll just be leaving you swelling with pride even as you try to hide your tears, an impossibly small baby hat clutched in one hand.

(*I'm not crying! You're crying!*)

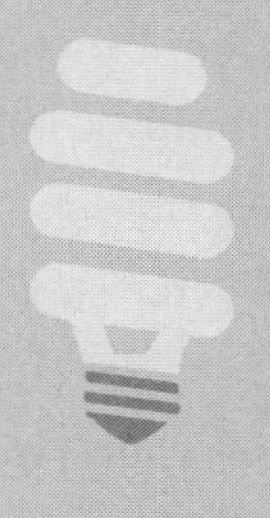

QUICK TIP

Even hippies have good manners. If you are given a gift that falls outside the boundaries of what you yourself would have chosen for your child, simply be gracious. It's one thing to offer gift guidelines to those near and dear to you, or if you are explicitly asked, but it is another thing entirely to refuse a gift or, worse, use the opportunity to climb up on your eco soapbox. I promise that the gifter did not intend to offend your environmental sensibilities, they just wanted to delight your child. Offer your warmest, most sincere thanks and leave it at that.

KEEP IT NEUTRAL

One way to ensure that you get as much use as you can out of each baby purchase is to try and buy it in a neutral color, rather than one that screams CARS! TRUCKS! BABY BOY! or FAIRY! PINK! PRINCESS!

I'm not trying to talk anyone out of those ridiculous flower headbands, or mini bow ties (seriously, who ever first put an infant in a bow tie should win a Nobel Peace Prize), but by keeping the bulk of your gear from crossing over into the pink/blue divide, you'll be able to use it again if you have a second or third child of a different gender, and you'll be able to cut down significantly on new purchases too.

Stick to getting strollers, car seats, swings and bouncers (if you have them at all) in gender-neutral colors. The same principle applies for clothing. If you keep basics in simple colors like red, yellow, green, white, beige, turquoise, etc., they can easily be worn by both genders. Stocking the bulk of baby's wardrobe in neutral colors makes it easily interchangeable among siblings, and you can always choose to add accessories that scream *boy* or *girl,* like shoes or the aforementioned headbands.

Alternately, you can stage a countercultural revolution in your child's closet by choosing to buck the notion of gendered colors altogether. Your baby won't care if he's wearing pink shoes, and does it really matter if a stranger at the park remarks how handsome your daughter is?

The idea that it's OK for girls to wear "boys'" clothing like pants or darker colors, but that the reverse—a little boy wearing a dress, or pinks and purples—is not, speaks to a darker truth about the value women hold in our society. If it is embarrassing to be wearing girls' clothing, it suggests that it is somehow understood (even among small children) that there is something inherently embarrassing about *being* a girl. That's a pretty harsh lesson to learn at three years old.

Who knew you could fight latent misogyny and teach a lesson about gender equality just by wearing a pair of Hello Kitty gloves?

You go, boy! Get your pink on.

POOP

This deserves a heading of its own, because approximately 60 percent of your time as a new parent will be thinking about, preparing for, or cleaning up after poop.

From that first strange tarry meconium poop, to the stressful stretches of time when they don't poop for days on end, to that one time where it shoots right out of their diaper and up into the folds of their neck, sometimes it seems like parenting is just one long poopy poop full of poop.

Due to its overwhelming presence in our lives, each and every parent has a poop story. At least I hope they do. I mean it wasn't just my parents who inflicted this strange sort of humiliation upon me, was it? My poop story is the time that my mother came to get me after a nap, only to find that I had smeared the contents of my diaper all over my blankets, my crib, and myself.

This story has been told dozens of times and, like the best tales, each time the story gets told there is more poop and more surfaces covered with poop. It gets exaggerated and multiplied and everyone has a good laugh at good ole poopy baby Madeleine.

Well, in an event so momentous that I'm a little miffed there's no spot for us to write it in her baby book, when Olive was three months old she got her very own poop story.

It begins with my reminding you that babies can't do anything for themselves. Including passing gas. (Is it indelicate to say "fart"? I have to say something other than "passing gas"; I'm not an elderly dowager. Is "toot" too cutesy? Whatever. We're talking about baby ~~farts~~ toots here. TOOTS it is!)

Anyway, you have to help them toot too. So there I was, changing our dear

Miss Olive, when she starts grunting and kicking in that telltale I'm-full-of-toots-please-help-me-Mama! way.

You will have to believe me when I say that she is an incredibly cute baby (and this from an incredibly biased source). So there I was, just having a time, looking deep into her gorgeous eyes and cooing at her, laughing at her funny facial expressions as I bicycled her legs and touched her toes to her nose, trying to release some of those pent-up toots.

Also, this is probably a good time to tell you, if you weren't aware already, that sometimes babies don't poop for many days. Yeah. This seems cool until you realize that they go from not pooping for a bunch of days in a row, to suddenly pooping eighteen days' worth all at once. In a massive poopsplosion. It's like a jack-in-the-box.

But with poop.

Do you see where this is going? Is that enough heavy-handed foreshadowing for you? If you see what's coming, you are smarter than I was.

I was getting quite a few toots while I was contorting her on that changing table, and I would be lying if I said that it wasn't making me extremely proud. I mean, it was like, "Look at this! I have mastered the problem of the Gassy Baby! I am supermom!"

Each fresh expulsion was like a little trumpet heralding my superior mothering abilities, my extreme competence.

And then, friends, this supermom bent her tiny daughter's legs one last time. She let out a particularly intense sort of grunty squeak, and I happened to look down and there it was. The Poop.

I didn't know what to do, I mean she hadn't done anything but pee in like five days, so I didn't want to jeopardize the situation, but, at the same time, she was pooping all over the changing table. My supreme mother confidence disappeared in an instant and, paralyzed by disbelief and horror, I just kept holding her legs by her head and she kept pooping and it was going on and on and on with no end in sight, and so, desperately, I started yelling, "Help! Adam! Help!"

Adam came whipping upstairs, probably expecting to see us in danger or in pain or both, but instead what he saw was his wife holding the legs of his infant daughter while poop flowed out of her like some sort of bizarre soft-serve machine gone horribly, horribly wrong.

He ran into the room and stood paralyzed with shock for one terrible moment as he took it all in. And then all hell broke loose. We both started panicking and yelling things like "Wipes!" and "Grab her feet!" and "Why god, *why?*" and "It's *everywhere!*"

And as we were yelling and panicking, she just kept going. Pooping! At one point Adam took her legs from me so I could grab some wipes and what can I say, we're rookies! It was a botched handoff and her body position was inadvertently shifted diagonally, which in turn moved her hand into reaching distance of the situation.

As I struggled to contain the poop with a series of wipes, she smacked one little hand into the rapidly forming pile and it splattered everywhere, and then she started waving it around and trying to grab onto Adam's arm.

"It's touching me!" Adam started shrieking, "Oh god, stop touching me! She's touching me with her poop hand!" and he was trying to get away from her, but he was still holding onto her legs so he couldn't get out of her reach and I was of zero assistance to him, this grown man being menaced by a tiny poop hand, because I was standing there with a fistful of wipes, doubled over with laughter and shaking so hard I could hardly see.

"Madeleine, help me!" Adam kept pleading, "She's touching me!"

And guys, *she just kept pooping*.

My god there was SO. MUCH. Looking back I'm strangely proud of her—where was she *hiding* it all? That strange combination of poop and pride: that's parenthood summed up right there.

The next few recipes will give you a few tips for dealing with the vast quantity of poop that is about to happen to you. Until you stumble upon your very own poop story, that is—you're on your own with that one.

Good luck.

(Number of times I said "poop" in this chapter: 38)

CLOTH DIAPERS

First, let me say that not using cloth diapers was never an option for us. This determination wasn't born of some over-inflated, holier-than-thou philosophy. (Hey, guys! My baby is better than your baby because she poops into fleece!) No, the decision was made simply because I wouldn't be able to handle the guilt of *not* doing it.

I don't know where it came from, this guilt, this crushing sense of failure if I throw something out that could have been recycled, or if I buy something new that could have been found secondhand. It just exists. Always. Heavy on my shoulders, whispering insidiously and steering me sternly toward hemp and recycled materials.

So for us the decision to do cloth diapers was already made. (Isn't it cute how I say "us" as if Adam had a say?) So we just needed to figure out which brand—and man, are there OPTIONS!

I realized pretty quickly that cloth diapering is much like everything else in baby land, it has its own jargon and its own fanatics, and it is complicated. You think you can just go somewhere and read about the different types of diapers, pick the one that best suits you, and be on your merry way? Wrong.

You read page after page, click on link after link, and each one leads you further than the last. Down, down, down the rabbit hole of information you go. Before you know it, you've spent five consecutive hours squinting at the computer screen while muttering about prefolds and liners, trying to make sense of nonsensical terms like snappis and bummis and huggabunz and rockin' green detergent. They talk about prepping and soaking and stripping, and trust me when I say that none of it is even a tiny bit as fun as it sounds.

Obviously, I went insane when I started researching this stuff. You haven't seen crazy until you've seen a seven-months-pregnant lady obsessing about all-in-ones vs. inserts. I researched and compared, read reviews and reports, and lost myself for weeks inside this strange and bewildering new world.

I did eventually managed to emerge with my sanity intact by letting my vanity choose for me by picking a brand with a little "g" on the bum. I thought that would be cool because our last name begins with a G. (Well, Adam's does. I feel that I should clarify this so that he doesn't feel the need to launch into the tragic tale of "Madeleine Didn't Take My Last Name Because She Doesn't Love Me," which he enjoys doing at random times and also when we are introducing ourselves to new couples who could have potentially become our friends, but now just think we are strange and maybe a little hostile too. Anyway, I'm going to stop talking about this, because I can move on. *Adam.*)

Cloth diapers are cheaper and generate less waste than disposables in the long run, especially if you plan on buying them secondhand or using them for more than one child. If you do choose cloth diapers, it's worth looking into local classifieds or diaper buy-and-sell groups to pick up a gently used set. Many people set out intending to cloth-diaper before discovering that it simply doesn't work for them, so there are often barely used diapers sets available for purchase at a deep discount. Just wash them on the hottest setting your washer has, in order to sanitize them before the first use.

There's no need to buy fancy cloth diaper detergent either. The homemade laundry detergent recipe on page 13 is great for diapers, gentle on baby's bum, and won't cause detergent buildup either.

Now in this, the age of the so-called mommy wars, I urge you to remember that cloth diapering doesn't work for everyone, so diaper changes are not the time to get your smug on. Despite the long-term savings, not everyone has the ability to cough up the initial chunk of cash needed to purchase cloth diapers, and if you don't have in-house laundry facilities the whole situation becomes pretty much impossible.

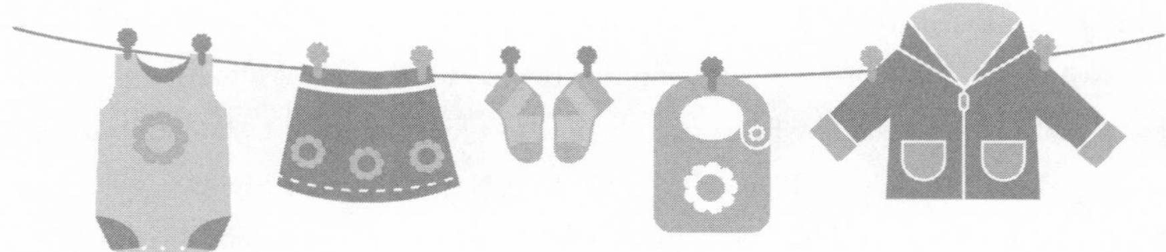

If either of these situations rings true for you, or if you're just not down with the idea of poop in your washing machine, there are several natural disposable diaper brands that offer recycled content, unbleached fibers, and less potentially harmful chemicals touching that sweet tush. Like most "green" choices offered in stores, however, they do tend to run a bit higher on the price scale but by choosing to buy secondhand, not buying superfluous baby items, and making many of your own things like baby food or wipes, you may be able to minimize the financial impact of choosing a greener diaper option altogether.

And here's another way of minimizing the impact of disposable diapers (and the water and energy used to wash cloth, for that matter): early potty training.

Yes. Early like, *early*: we're talking starting the process before age one. Don't look at me like that! I have it on good authority that, back in the day, babies used to start potty training at around three months, with the 1946 Dr. Sears parenting book advising parents to *delay* potty training until six months![17] Evidence is growing that it's possible to toilet-train babies far earlier than conventionally thought with no ill-effects, and if you're willing to invest the time it's possible to save on the cost and waste of hundreds of diapers altogether.

There are many resources available on the subject, and as always the Internet contains a wealth of information and support, should you choose to go this route. As an added bonus, and I speak from experience here, there is absolutely nothing cuter than a seven-month-old sitting on a tiny potty.

BABY SKIN CARE

Baby skin is possibly the most incredible thing ever. Smooth, plump, and soft as velvet. It's is the Holy Grail, the pinnacle of beauty that we all seem to be trying to turn back the clock to try to attain. Every single cosmetic company and skincare line out there is trying to convince you that you can achieve the dewy glow of a baby's cheeks with their special lotions and potions.

There are many products on the market marketed as safe for that pristine baby skin—shampoos, body washes, bubble baths, and lotions. And if you have read this far it should come as no surprise that I advise you to buy exactly *none* of them.

Your baby's skin needs very little interference. I mean, have you *felt* it? Why mess with perfection?

So what do you do? AS LITTLE AS POSSIBLE.

- Bathe your baby only every second day or so, to ensure that her skin doesn't get too dried out.
- The only product you truly need is a bit of natural, fragrance-free soap to clean your little one when he needs it, and oftentimes just rinsing with bathwater is enough.
- Most babies really don't need lotion or moisturizer, but if you like to use it for baby massage or if your little guy has dry skin, 1–2 drops of lavender essential oil mixed into 1 cup of coconut oil creates a naturally relaxing, baby-friendly moisturizer.

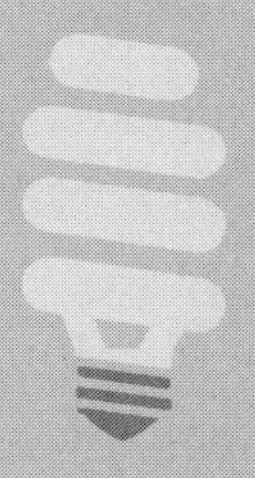

QUICK TIP

Although essential oils are natural, they can still be irritating to skin, especially sensitive baby skin. To prevent irritation, use sparingly, never apply directly to skin, and *always* blend well into a carrier oil.

MAKE IT

Belly butter

I took weekly pictures of myself throughout my pregnancy. Every Tuesday I would cram myself into a pink dress, strike a pose in my hallway, and snap a shot of my growing belly.

I felt ridiculous each and every time I crammed myself into that dress—which stretched an obscene amount through those weeks—and stood there trying to minimize my double chins before the shutter snapped. Looking back, however, I am so, *so* glad I did this, if only to laugh at my complete and total naiveté.

Seriously, I was an idiot.

On the day I was fifteen weeks pregnant, I wrote on my blog:

"The past week has been the most physically challenging of my pregnancy thus far. It's the first time I've felt uncomfortable in my body, like I'm being pushed out, stretched somehow… I am beginning to feel heavy and cumbersome. Obtrusive."

FIFTEEN WEEKS.

Oh god, I'm laughing so hard I think I might have just peed a little bit. LOOK AT ME. I actually used the words cumbersome and obtrusive. With a straight face. To describe a bump that you have to squint to see!

I should have known better. I should have saved those ridiculous adjectives for twenty-one weeks later, when I really had an obtrusive belly.

It never ceases to amaze me how my body was able to effortlessly stretch and grow, how it became round and full. It was an incredible feat, and, even amidst my ridiculous musings at fifteen weeks, I knew that I had to do whatever I could to help my body ease into that transition from a (somewhat) flat stomach to a big mixing-bowl belly.

Everyone will tell you that there's no definitive evidence that topical creams are effective at preventing stretch marks, but I think this is due to a complete lack of studies on the subject. Studies are lacking in part because scientists are too busy doing important things like finding cures for fatal diseases, but also because individual differences in skin elasticity mean that, in order to get accurate results, women would have to be willing to treat half their belly with a cream that claims to prevent stretch marks, and leave the other half bare—running the risk of ending up with a belly that looks like Two-Face from Batman.

Who would do that?

Exactly.

So we have no proof that they work, but we also don't know that they *don't* work, and—who knows?—maybe the placebo effect can work its magic on belly skin too. Thus, illogical reasoning in place, I chose to err on the safe side and lather up.

I am reluctant to stray into the fear-mongering tone found in almost every piece of literature aimed at pregnant women. (Did you know? That spoon you're holding may be TOTALLY TOXIC! I mean, it's *probably* not. But, here is some halfway scientific mumbo-jumbo and spurious conjecture, just enough to strike fear into your crazy pregnant heart. If you love your baby *at all* you should avoid using spoons yourself and don't go near anyone *else* using a spoon, and, in fact, just steer clear of *all* utensils just to be safe. You can jab at your food with a blunt chopstick instead!)

Nonetheless, you *are* growing a little person inside of you, and unfortunately all those magazine articles and opinionated old ladies at the grocery store are kind of right. Pregnancy is a time to be especially careful about what you're putting on your skin—and it's even more reason to opt for natural products.

There are several natural belly butters out there, and, if you want to buy one, look for something that is paraben-, phlalate-, and fragrance-free. This could mean a trip to CosmeticsDatabase.com to check up on the ingredients in store-bought brands, or of course you could just make your own.

Coconut oil is a great option for moisturizing your bump, but some may find it too light to banish the crazy belly-itches that can plague you in the second and third trimesters.

For a rich, emollient cream that works well on dry hands and feet too, mix an equal amount of shea butter and coconut oil together in a small bowl and stir well. Shea butter is a fat derived from the shea nut, making it a luxurious moisturizer. You can typically find it in health food stores—just make sure it's 100 percent pure and unrefined. Melting the coconut oil a bit can help the two combine.

After mixing your concoction, you can add a few drops of your favorite essential oils if you like (lavender and bergamot are nice). A relaxing scent makes moisturizing your belly a great way to relax and connect with the little person hanging out inside.

Baby wipes

Hypothetical question for you: Have you ever gone to the bathroom at a friend's house and found yourself staring at an empty toilet paper roll?

Maybe you look under the sink and above the toilet, but in all the usual places there's no spare roll in sight, and you start to panic a bit, thinking "Oh my gosh, I'm going to be stuck on the toilet forever, I'll never be able to leave and they'll wonder what happened to me and eventually they'll forget my name and I'll be known only as "Toilet Lady" and they'll have to bring me my meals and oh my *god,* I'm going to be eating macaroni and cheese with my pants around my ankles forever and ever and normally that would sound kind of awesome but not under these conditions—not now!"

Then, maybe, did you start to freak out and even cry a little bit because damn, you don't *want* to be Toilet Lady, and then did you all of a sudden find a solution that would prevent you from becoming Toilet Lady and did that solution just so happen to be a package of baby wipes?

No? That's never happened to you? Really?

I mean, of course not—right? Me neither!

Ha! Oh wow. Awkward.

ANYWAY, if I *had* ever found myself in that rather awkward situation (which I totally *haven't*), I think I would probably tell you that those baby wipes are NOT pleasant on your tender lady bits—not at all. And this experience, this COMPLETELY hypothetical experience, makes me wonder why we are using these wipes on the tender bits and pieces of our littlest ones.

So to replace these (allegedly) irritating store-bought baby wipes, there are two options: we can make disposable ones ourselves, or use cloth wipes with a homemade wipe solution.

Disposable wipes

I'll start with the disposable wipes.

With this method we're still generating waste, but by making the wipes ourselves we can reduce a lot of the packaging involved, as well as limiting the amount of weird and (not so) wonderful mystery ingredients we're putting on our babes.

TO MAKE DISPOSABLE BABY WIPES YOU WILL NEED:

1 sealable container large enough to fit a paper-towel roll cut in half

1 roll of recycled paper towels

2 cups of water, boiled and cooled

2 tablespoons Dr. Bronner's Castile soap

1 tablespoon olive oil

Start by using a serrated knife to cut the paper towel roll in half. Place one half inside your container.

In a medium-sized bowl mix the water, the Castile soap, and the olive oil. The reason that we boil and cool the water is to ensure that it's sterile.

When the mixture is combined well, pour it over the paper towels, close the container, and then shake, rattle, and roll it around until the liquid is fully absorbed.

Wait a half-hour or so, and then open the container, remove the inner cardboard tube, and pull your first wipe from the inside of the roll.

All done! These wipes are quick, inexpensive, and totally simple to make. Your baby's butt will be clean, sweet-smelling, and smooth to the touch. And, best of all, you know *exactly* what ingredients went into getting it that way.

Cloth wipes

If you'd prefer to use cloth wipes, you need only look around you to find the materials to get started. Fine washcloths, sheets, or any sort of soft absorbent cloth that's not being used anymore. (Jersey-knit sheets or T-shirts are ideal for this type of thing because they don't require any sewing and won't unravel.)

Run the material through the wash on a hot cycle to make sure the cloth is clean and pre-shrunk, then measure out and cut into a uniform size. Squares measuring 8 inches x 8 inches will fold neatly into a wipe container, but you can make them any size you like.

When the wipes are done, just pile them in a basket on the changing table and they're ready to go. Wash in hot water, and dry in the sun to remove any stains or odor.

If you are a compulsive closet-purger (ahem) and you don't have any material hanging around that would be suitable for wipes, you can choose to support someone in your community, or someone on Etsy, by purchasing cloth wipes instead. I'm lucky enough that my crafty sister Claire kindly whipped some up for me.

The benefits of reusable wipes are endless. If they are washed on a hot cycle, they can do double duty as baby washcloths or burp cloths, and can be kept and reused for the next baby in the family.

Baby-wipe solution

If you've decided to use cloth wipes, you can make this solution to take the edge off those messy diaper cleanups. The Castile soap is a gentle cleanser with a natural scent, aloe helps soothe baby's bum, and olive oil allows the mixture to glide easily and moisturize that tender tush.

INGREDIENTS

4 cups water, boiled and cooled

3 tablespoons olive oil

2 tablespoons Dr. Bronner's Castile soap

3 teaspoons pure aloe vera

Pour all the ingredients into a large jar and measure out into a squeeze bottle as needed (a well-rinsed shampoo or dish detergent bottle works great for this).

The olive oil will rise to the top of the bottle between uses but don't panic, that's normal. Just give it a shake before you use it and you're good to go.

QUICK TIP

- Most of the ingredients above will be a snap to find. The only one that may give you trouble is the aloe. It can often be found in health food stores as a sunburn relief treatment. Just make sure to get 100 percent pure aloe vera. Some products feature a smaller amount blended into an emollient cream—you want 100 percent of the good stuff, so check the label.

- If you are reading this and thinking, "Listen, lady, I don't have time to run around on some wild goose chase in search of pure aloe! For god's sake, I just had a BABY!" then first I'd like to suggest that you sit down and have a small glass of wine. Then I'd like to let you know that you can leave the aloe out altogether if you can't find it, or heck, just use plain old water

- Better yet, delegate this whole shebang to your partner or a helpful relative with some time to kill. They'll feel important, and you can finally get some sleep already and stop yelling at books. Sheesh.

Diaper rash cream

There are approximately a bazillion diaper creams on the market, and the only one I've ever had to use is coconut oil. It's simple, quick and safe for baby. Rub a bit on after a diaper change and baby's butt will stay smooth, soft, and diaper rash free!

CHAPTER 9
Pet

YOUR DOG DOES NOT NEED A SWEATER (OR A STROLLER) (OR BOOTS)

When we first got Gus, our adorable chubby English Mastiff puppy, we had a few rules. He wasn't going to be allowed on the furniture, we would never give him people food (especially not right off of our plates), and we definitely, definitely weren't going to go crazy getting him all sorts of useless *stuff.*

Cut to five years later. Adam sits on our dog-hair-covered couch, sneaking Gus pieces of salmon from his plate. In our basement lives a box containing the following: a doggie life jacket, a harness, a rain jacket, puppy boots, various toys, balls, ropes, etc., three brushes, and two alternate collars, including a Velcro one that's designed to look like a shirt collar and black tie (for special occasions).

So. That went well.

I must admit that, in our defense, much of this was purchased for Gus by loving family and friends, but I have no one but myself to blame for the black tie. Gus made an appearance at our wedding, and I thought that if our guests had to put up with drool on their dress shoes, the least the guy could do was dress up a bit.

Nonetheless, looking back, I wish I could un-buy 70 percent of what we bought Gus. Not only because my attitudes toward waste have changed, or because I'm trying to live a more sustainable life, but because Gus truly didn't need any of what we got him. With dogs, as with babies, I find that the majority of our purchases are meant to satisfy our wants or needs, instead of theirs.

Yes, Gus loved the cool ball that whistled when we threw it. He loved the chew toys and the funky patterned dog bed and the tug-of-war rope that he ate piece by piece over the course of a few weeks. But he would have been just as happy without them.

I mean, have you ever *met* a dog? Every single day is the best day of their life. You let them outside in the morning: best day ever! You feed them: best day ever! You take them to the dog park where they let a rambunctious chocolate lab debase them for fifteen minutes straight: best day ever!

So while I can't deny that Gus enjoyed the toys we got him, I truly think he would have been just as happy swimming with us in a cool lake, followed by a long belly rub. He truly couldn't care less about cute collars or black ties, and though his dog bed is comfy, he's way happier when we let him sneak into our room at night and sleep on the floor beside our bed.

Also: dogs are animals. I just thought I'd mention that because they are so adorable and have such huge personalities, and we project so much of our desires and feelings and fashion dreams onto them, that it is very easy to forget.

Further to this point, dogs don't need stuff. We buy them things that we think will make them happy, but what they really need is us. Training, walks, and affection. That's all. No cash required. And, in fact, the less we buy, the more money is left in our pocket, which means we might be able to work a little less and play fetch a little more.

Beyond the fact that I think we can all admit that dogs do not know, or care, if they are wearing a little sweater, the things we buy for them often have an incredibly short life span. Clothing doesn't last long before becoming soiled or torn, and any plastic toys that come within drooling distance of big Gus end up as brightly colored plastic confetti within a matter of days.

A better option to spoil your pooch that the pups seem to be quite fond of too is to buy edible treats that leave nothing to toss in the garbage or clog up your vacuum. Gus has never been happier than when we hand him a monstrous raw bone to chew. He lies in the backyard, holds in between his front paws, and will be there for hours. It's great for his teeth, the meat and marrow are far more nutritious than the furry covering of a tennis ball, and there's very little waste.

When I think to the future, if I allow myself the unthinkable task of imagining our world without Gus, at a time when we might be contemplating getting a new dog, I will have more realistic rules: He will be allowed on the furniture for snuggles on movie nights. We will share tidbits of meat off of our plates if he agrees not to soak our feet with drool while he waits for it. And we definitely, *definitely* aren't going to go crazy getting him a bunch of *stuff*.

For real this time.

MAKE IT

Stinky dog spray

Fill a small spray bottle with hot water, and dissolve 1–2 tablespoons of baking soda. Add 1 tablespoon oil (olive, sesame, jojoba, etc.) and 20–25 drops of your favorite essential oil.

The baking soda helps neutralize pet odors, while the oil moisturizes their coat. Essential oils camouflage any lingering stink. Spray liberally anywhere pooch likes to hang out, as well as on the offending animal itself.

Pet bed

While we are incredibly lucky that Gus was never a chewer (can you imagine the damage those jaws would do? With a dog this big we would be talking about more than just slippers), but due to his size and his love of long ocean dips he is perpetually stinky, no matter how much we bathe him. This makes it essential that his dog bed be washable so that I can toss it in the laundry each week to keep the smell to a minimum.

When we first got him, we bought a huge dog bed that had a removable zippered cover, and I would happily take it off each week and wash it. Dirt and stink were cut to a minimum, Gus was happy, I was happy—everything was great!

And then he started smelling like the swamp thing, and then our house started smelling like the swamp thing, and I couldn't figure out why my whole life was going to hell in a swamp basket until one day I was removing his dog bed cover and happened to sniff the insert inside and, guys, I died.

I was laid flat by the horrific mix of wet dog and fishy ocean and musty fusty malodorous stink. It wasn't just the cover that stunk, but the entire pillow *insert* too. And it didn't matter how much I washed Gus, or washed his bed cover, because the odorific insert was contaminating everything.

This is why I can't have nice things.

The insert itself was made of tiny foam strips and couldn't be washed. I couldn't bear to throw the whole thing out, so my make-do solution was to sprinkle the offending insert with baking soda, then wrap it in a sheet so that it might buffer the smell and I could at least wash that, but I've since discovered something that would stop this problem from ever starting, and am kicking myself for not doing this in the first place. Perhaps you can benefit from my mistake.

Instead of getting a pet bed filled with foam strips, or cotton batting or those horrible little Styrofoam balls, just purchase a dog bed cover (readily found with some quick Googling, in tons of cute designs), and a mesh laundry bag roughly the same size as the pet bed.

Stuff the mesh bag with old clothes, towels, or rags that you're not using anymore, to form the filling of the bed. It's an incredibly easy solution that cleans out your closets while also letting you just toss the whole deal in the washing machine every week or so. A nice, sweet-smelling bed for Fluffy or Fido or, yes, even big Gus.

Flea spray

Fleas are horrid, and I prefer to think about them as little as possible so I'm going to keep this short and sweet.

If you'd like to try an alternative to conventional flea prevention methods, use Apple Cider Vinegar instead. Add a teaspoon to your pet's water, and spritz their fur, bedding, collar etc. with a solution of 1 part ACV with 1 part water.

The vinegar works well to repel and prevent fleas without smearing a chemical cocktail all over your furry friend.

Pet toothpaste

The recipe for making pet toothpaste is pretty much identical to the one we made for you back in the second chapter, but you'll increase the chances of your pooch staying still for longer than three seconds if you replace the peppermint flavoring with beef or chicken.

COMBINE:

⅔ cup baking soda

1–2 tablespoons beef or chicken broth

Slowly add the broth to the baking soda until you get a nice thick slurry. Once you've reached the desired consistency the real fun begins—dip a pet toothbrush into the mixture and then prepare to wrestle your hound for access to those fangs.

I am proud to say that when Gus and I engage in this battle I almost always emerge victorious (and by "victorious," I mean sweaty and covered in beef-flavored drool).

LITTER BOX TIPS FOR SEXY CAT LADIES

The Internet has been the best thing to happen to cats since they were made into demigods in ancient Egypt. Never before have they enjoyed such fame or popularity, and yet despite their almost universal appeal, for reasons unbeknownst to me, the crazy cat-lady stereotype persists.

You know the one: the lonely, bored spinster who uses cats as bizarre sort of stand-ins for real fulfilling human relationships, and occasionally as projectiles when she stands on her porch in curlers, screeching obscenities at neighborhood children.

I'm not sure how this stereotype persists, especially given that fully 40 percent of the entire Internet is devoted to pictures of Grumpy Cat, and 50 percent to videos of adorable kittens chasing laser pointers and getting stuck in boxes. (Leaving, of course, the remaining 10 percent for porn and Facebook.) (Are you questioning my statistics? Guys, don't shoot the messenger, these are FACTS.)

(These are not facts)

I don't think there's anything crazy about cat ladies. I think they are smart, sexy women who happen to enjoy the company of one (or two, or three, or fourteen) feline friends.

Despite my support, however, I must admit that I am not now, nor have I ever been, a cat lady. I like cats, and I've always gotten along famously with our family cat, Oliver, a dapper fellow who once woke me up by sitting on my chest and drooling into my mouth—I mean really, what's not to like about that?

I like to think that Oliver's little drool bath made me an honorary cat lady, but in the interests of full disclosure I must tell you that these are the only recipes in the book that I don't regularly use. I briefly debated trying to teach Gus to use a litter box so that I could test them, but thankfully some sexy cat lady friends stepped in and volunteered to be guinea pigs for a good cause.

When they found out I was writing this book, they made me promise to include some cat-friendly tips, and wanting nothing more than to please these smart, witty, and utterly *desirable* women (that's me doing my part to eradicate the stereotype), I got to researching.

The two things bugging cat people everywhere were:

1. Is there some magic I can employ to stop my cat from shedding? Like...*forever*?
2. What can I do about this whole nasty litter box situation?

SHEDDING

Look, if I had a way to stop animals from shedding, I would be rich. RICH! More importantly, my house, my clothing, my car, and my baby would not be perpetually clothed in a thick layer of dog hair.

But alas, I am sorry to say that I have no hippie magic that can stop your pet from shedding altogether. The best you can hope for here is to simply minimize the collateral damage. Set aside some time each week for regular grooming, vacuuming, and praying to the gods and goddesses above that your pet becomes suddenly, prematurely bald.

For getting rid of hair on clothing and furniture, choose one of the fancy red-velvet-looking lint brushes, rather than the rollers that rely on sticky strips to pick up hair. By doing this you can neatly sidestep buying (and throwing out) all those little adhesive sheets, and, generally speaking, the brushes work just as well and are even great on upholstery too.

I recommend keeping one in your front hall closet to give yourself a quick swipe as you head out the door in the morning and also one in your glove box for those inevitable moments where you realize that somehow in the five steps it took you to get from your doorstep to your car, you have become covered in hair all over again.

(*Stifled scream.*)

To take care of loose pet hair around the house, a dust mop like the one I described on pages 29–30 is your best friend here. It works particularly well to capture all those furry tumbleweeds rolling around your floors.

For carpet there's nothing better than a vacuum with a good beater bar, but if you own animals you probably knew that already, and, really, this is all common sense and I think as I am writing this and you are reading this we are both coming to the terrible realization that pets shed (*a lot*) and there is literally nothing we can do about it. We have no control.

I'm sorry.

Now! On the litter box front I *do* have suggestions. Helpful suggestions! You will want to hug me and kiss me and maybe even drool into my mouth a little bit.

Read on, sexy cat ladies, read on.

THE LITTER BOX

I think we can all agree that waste disposal is, paws down, the most unpleasant part of owning a pet. Gus has the decency to poop outside, where I am able to turn a blissful blind eye to the whole horrid situation until I can swindle my nephews into pooper-scooping (thanks, Liam and Jett!), but, as they will tell you, it's no picnic.

Similarly, I'm utterly powerless to change the basic fact that collecting your cat's excrement in a little box in your bathroom is nobody's idea of a good time, but hopefully these tips can make dealing with it a bit easier (and a bit more earth-friendly too).

First of all, we need to talk about the actual litter itself. If you are using clay litter or clumping litter or fancy expensive perfumed litter, your darling kitty is most likely stepping into a big box o' chemicals every time she needs to poop. Then she's tracking those chemical particulates all over your couch, countertops, and lap, as well as ingesting them when she grooms herself, which can contribute to serious health problems down the road. Plus, none of that litter biodegrades, and that means that each year, literally millions of pounds of cat litter ends up being dumped into the landfill and just sitting there. *Forever.*

Are you feeling guilty yet, sexy cat ladies? Good. GOOD. I know I said at the beginning of this book that I wasn't going to guilt-trip you, but I lied a little bit.

Don't be angry, because this is for your own good. Trust me, you will need this guilt to power through that faint feeling you will get standing in the kitty litter aisle and looking at the prices of natural kitty litters.

I know, I KNOW. Bear with me, OK?

In terms of natural kitty litters, you have a few different options when searching for alternatives to the typical clay-based kind. I'm a fan of the newspaper-based "Yesterday's News," which is literally just little pellets of compressed newspaper. It is usually priced a tiny bit above conventional litters, but it utilizes recycled materials and is relatively dust-free. We used it for our bunnies with great success, but one cat lady told me that it doesn't eliminate odors as well as conventional litters, which can sometimes be the downside of giving up those mysterious chemical compounds. Mixing ¼ cup of baking soda in with the litter will do a lot to help to keep the odor down, but if you are sensitive to smell, live in a small place, or have multiple cats, this might not be the best solution for you.

The second natural litter option is to use a brand that employs coarsely ground whole wheat instead of clay. The gluten in wheat helps create that clumping action that makes poop so easy to scoop, and you get all the convenience of a conventional kitty litter without the potential chemical side effects.

Both these options offer a natural alternative to conventional kitty litters with the same convenience, at a slightly higher price. But if you like a good challenge, or just have more time than you do money, you could always try making your own versions of the natural kitty litters described above.

It'll take a little longer than driving to the store to buy a bag pre-made, but if you do a few batches at once it'll save time, as well as a ton of cash.

(It's not as ridiculous as it sounds.)

(OK, it kind of is. But think of the *children!*)

MAKE IT

DIY newspaper kitty litter

Two options here. One is to simply shred newspaper and use it in place of regular kitty litter. This is quick and cheap, but probably best used in a home with a single cat or an outdoor cat that only uses the litter box periodically.

The other option is a little more labor-intensive but the payoff is that it's more effective too. This recipe comes from Allie at AlliesAnswers.com, and it involves essentially pulping and drying newspaper to make your own alternative to newspaper-based litter. You should be able to make enough for a two- or three-week supply in under an hour.

SUPPLIES

Paper shredder

Screen

Large container

DIRECTIONS

1. First, shred enough newspaper to fill your litter box heaping full. This is a great way to recycle newspaper or those free weekly papers that seem to multiply on street corners. NO glossy paper, though.
2. Dump the whole thing in warm water mixed with a few squirts of biodegradable dish soap. The soap helps to lift some of the ink and prevent it from coating kitty's paws.

The shredded paper will take on a cooked oatmeal consistency, and while the newspaper won't come completely clean, the water will turn gray.

3. Drain the water using a sieve or colander and repeat the soaking process minus the soap.
4. Drain again, and then sprinkle baking soda liberally on the wet paper. Knead it into the mixture (wear gloves to avoid getting ink on your hands).
5. Squeeze the remaining moisture out until it's as dry as you can get it.
6. Spread it out onto a screen (this is a great use for an old window screen or broken screen door). Leave the mixture to dry, which will take 1–2 days.

This is a great hands-on project that kids would really enjoy, and doing it outside when possible will cut down on the mess significantly. The process is simple enough to make bulk quantities at once, so you may only have to do it once a month.

The only downside to making your own kitty litter is that having your neighbor see you washing newspaper and then setting it out to dry isn't going to do much to help that whole crazy cat lady thing you've got going on.

Sorry.

DIY wheat litter

Several natural kitty litters use finely ground whole wheat in place of clay. The wheat is great for keeping odors down, it's usually compostable (check the guidelines in your local municipality), and, if you can track down feed-grade bulk wheat kernels, it'll be less than half the cost of buying the litter itself.

What you're looking for is wheat kernels, sometimes called wheat berries. You'd probably be able to find them in health food stores, or even the bulk section of some grocery stores, but they'll be food-grade wheat and you might end up paying more than if you just bought the litter pre-made, and what's the point of that?

Instead, look for animal-grade wheat kernels. If you are in a rural area, call around to local feed stores to see if they carry them or head to the almighty Internet to search for an online supplier.

If you are buying the kernels whole, just pop them into a grinder or food processor until they resemble rough sawdust, then use as you would conventional litter.

Bingo! Easy, biodegradable do-it-yourself solutions for your pretty kitty's poop.

GENERAL LITTER BOX TIPS

- The more often you scoop, the less often you will have to do an entire litter-box overhaul. Regular maintenance goes a long way here.
- After emptying the box, wash it well with Castile soap or dish soap, and then rinse with white vinegar to eliminate any lingering cat-pee ammonia smell.
- After a thorough scrub-down but before loading up with fresh litter, give your litter box a wipe with olive or canola oil. Just like greasing a baking pan, putting down a slick layer of oil acts as a barrier to prevent soiled litter from sticking to the bottom of the box and making clean-up easier in the future.
- If you do switch to a natural kitty litter and you're not composting it, make sure you're using biodegradable bags to toss it in the trash; otherwise all that lovely natural stuff will just be stuck inside a plastic prison forever and ever and ever. (Actually it's a good idea to switch all your garbage bags to a biodegradable brand for the same reason.)

CHAPTER 10

Holidays

HOW TO CURB HOLIDAY EXCESS WITHOUT BECOMING A SCROOGE

Every Christmas, after the rip and tear is over and every last one of my five siblings lies bloated and exhausted from the tryptophan and the excitement, I lie alongside them feeling a crush of guilt settle in around my shoulders.

It's something about the excess, I think. The overwhelming excess of love, and family, and wrapping, and gifts, and, yes, the excess of garbage too.

In some ways this humble, somewhat guilty feeling is nice, it makes me feel lucky—if undeserving—to have such a close family, such lavish meals and thoughtful gifts. But, in other ways, when I look at the amount of *stuff* bought and waste generated, it just feels kind of hollow.

This feeling has begun settling in amongst the shoulders of others too in recent years, and in spite of—or perhaps in response to—a consumer culture that is always pushing for MORE! and BIGGER! and NEWER!, a small resistance seems to be forming. A shift toward quality, not quantity, and small thoughtful gifts, rather than piles upon piles of plastic crap.

In a happy coincidence, both Adam's family and my own made this very shift about five years ago.

We are both fortunate enough to have large, close-knit families: my five siblings and their ever-growing numbers of partners, plus Adam's two siblings and *their* partners, and four nieces and nephews to boot. By the time the dust settled each holiday season we were looking at buying twenty-six individual gifts once we included our four-legged friends, as well as small gifts for each other.

That's a lot of time spent finding a perfect gift for each person, a lot of angry screaming at slow walkers in mall parking lots, a lot of fussing with wrapping paper, and I mean—*holy moley*—a lot of money too! The whole thing was exhausting and overwhelming, as was being on the receiving end of all those gifts. No one needs that much stuff!

Eventually both families decided to stop getting a gift *for* each person and *from* each person, and started doing a Secret Santa-style gift exchange instead, where the names of each family member (excluding kids) go into a hat, and you draw to see whom you're buying a gift for. It was the best thing we ever did. This one *tiny* change cut the total present count down from twenty-six to ten.

Doing a Secret Santa-style gift exchange for any holiday where gifts are exchanged is a great way to refocus the priority of get-togethers back to family rather than gifts, without eliminating them altogether. It also allows you to devote time to finding something well-made, useful, and perfectly suited to your giftee, rather than falling into the haphazard, last-minute "this'll do" style of gift giving.

(As for what exactly you should get for those ten people you still have to shop for, page 170 has some great gift suggestions that don't involve tangible things.)

For those of you who celebrate Christmas there is the added challenge of filling stockings. Don't get sucked in by the checkout counter displays of "Stocking Stuffers," which are usually just a bunch of cheap trinkets and baubles designed to fill space. Instead, find useful items like toiletries, books, or small consumable indulgences. (I mean, who *wouldn't* want to find a tiny bottle of Baileys in their stocking?) (CHILDREN! That's who, you monster.)

And finally, try to curb the amount of waste by collecting wrapping paper for reuse or recycling (yes, I am asking you to be that guy neatly unwrapping his gift and folding the paper for later) or using the suggestions on page 245 for alternatives to wrapping paper altogether.

Use real dishes and cutlery instead of paper and plastic, and consider dialing back the over-the-top light displays. Mother Earth (and your sleep-deprived neighbors) will thank you.

Gift-giving to children can also spiral out of control rather quickly, and it's not hard to see why. Their clothing is adorable, their excitement upon opening a much-desired toy is infectious, and everyone so desperately wants to make their holiday a memorable one.

Kids are funny, though, because, whether they receive five gifts or fifteen, they will typically end up with one or two favorites that are played with nonstop, while the rest get abandoned after a few uses (and you just *know* that one of those favorites will end up being a cardboard box).

While Secret Santa exchanges don't typically work well with kids unless they are old enough to select and pay for gifts themselves, many parents have started either giving one gift per child, or sticking to the rule of "One gift you want, one you need, one gift to wear, and one to read."

By using this handy rhyme, instead of receiving enough toys to start their own small toy store your child will get one toy, something they *actually* need (like a helmet, or a recorder for upcoming music lessons), one new item of clothing, and a book.

Doing Want/Need/Wear/Read gifts can cut down on excessive gift giving while also teaching children the difference between wants and needs, the importance of practical gifts, and the value of reading.

Just remember not to go overboard. I mean, the whole point of managing the excessiveness of gifts isn't to become some holiday miser counting your pennies and begrudging your family their presents—really, in the grand scheme of things, too many loved ones to shop for is kind of an awesome problem to have.

Instead, the point is to gently shift the focus of celebrations away from gifts in order to focus more on celebrating togetherness in the cheesiest, most Walton-esque way, as well as reducing the amount of environmental pollution and consumerism to boot.

MAKE IT

Wrapping paper

Excess is as intrinsic to holidays as family drama. After all, what is Thanksgiving without collapsing into a bloated couch-coma, or New Year's Day without the cruel remains of a raging champagne hangover?

Christmas, however, is the most excessive of all, and while we've been over some tips to reduce the excessiveness of the gifts themselves, we're now going to tackle how they're wrapped. (Needless to say, this tip applies to all gifts, not just those given at Christmas, but I'd wager that this is when the bulk of wrapping waste is generated).

It's pretty simple, really: stop using wrapping paper.

I mean, if you have some left over in your stash definitely use it up, but if you are thinking about going out and buying new wrapping paper this year, I have a ton of other cute, creative, earth-friendly options to try instead.

What can you use in place of wrapping paper? Oh, just about anything, including (but not limited to):

- Colorful cloth scraps
- Newspaper
- A reusable bag
- Maps (especially great for going-away parties)
- A cute new tea towel
- Or even those shirts of your husband's you've been trying

to get rid of for three years (cut them up first so he can't steal them back).

Although I've used each of these options at some point (sorry, Adam), newspaper is always my go-to solution. It's inexpensive and plentiful and offers a neutral background that's easy to dress up with colorful ribbons, raffia, paint, or felt pens.

I usually use the funny pages for wrapping children's gifts, and have used yarn and buttons in place of bows in the past.

Just be aware that you may have to select your wrapping pages judiciously or you will end up like my five-year-old niece, who had an ad for a liquor store on the front of her gift last Christmas.

Awkward (but what a deal on that Baileys!).

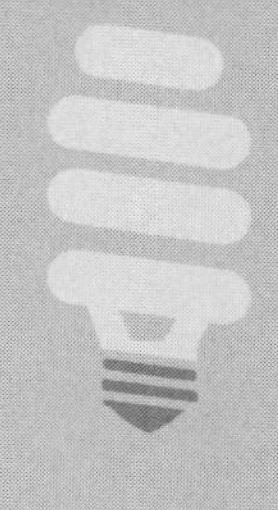

QUICK TIP

When it's time to go for ice cream, use a cone instead of a cup. Even if you don't end up eating the cone, you'll come out ahead by not wasting a little dish. Plus, eating ice cream the old fashioned way with that complex system of licking, rotating, and avoiding those sneaky drips is probably better for your brain than crossword puzzles. (Added bonus: foreplay?)

Recycled paper gift bow

Once I learned to make these I was hooked! It seems a bit tricky at first but once you get the hang of it you'll be able to make these with your eyes closed.

SUPPLIES

Magazine pages, or any paper cut to letter size

Ruler

Scissors

Stapler/Tape

DIRECTIONS

Cut the magazine page into 9 strips, each ¾ inches wide. Leave the first three strips full length, then cut one inch off of the second three strips, two inches off of the next two, and cut the last one to 3 inches long.

YOU SHOULD END UP WITH:

3 strips full height

3 strips with an inch cut off

2 strips with 2 inches cut off

1 strip cut down to 3 inches

The first three full-length strips are going to form the widest base of your bow. Taking one in your hand, twist the strip to create loops on both ends (like an infinity symbol, or an awareness ribbon).

Staple or tape in the middle to secure the loops. Repeat this process for all the strips except the 3-inch one.

Assemble the loops, layering them in an offset pattern: the three largest as the base, then the three medium, then the two small. Staple or tape into place.

Curl the 3-inch piece into a circle and secure in the middle of your bow with tape or staples.

Ta-da! A gorgeous recycled bow! This is truly the perfect accessory to a gift wrapped in newsprint.

This craft can also be a great use for your child's artwork—let your little one proudly attach the finished product to gifts destined for friends, family, or teachers.

QUICK TIP

Invest in some reusable decorations for birthdays and other small holidays that you can use year after year. Fabric banners, felt hearts, and cloth tablecloths are inexpensive and more durable than the cheap party-store stuff you have to replace every year.

Make a difference

The thing about holidays is that they are these magical times of family, and togetherness, and making memories that will last lifetimes.

Until, of course, they're not.

If you've recently divorced or separated or lost a loved one; if your life doesn't currently have those qualities of family and togetherness and magic memory-making; or even if you don't celebrate a particular holiday for reasons of religion, or reason, or simple rebellious dissent—if any of these apply to you, you already know that sometimes the holidays aren't fun, they're horrible.

It's not just one day. It's *endless.* You have to hear about the holiday for weeks in advance as advertising campaigns are rolled out and store displays get unfurled and radio stations are suddenly all playing the same songs. Everyone is talking about the holiday and their plans for the holiday and how fabulous the holiday is going to be and you just feel like shouting "Eff this stupid mother-effing holiday!" But you don't, of course. (Right?)

Amidst all the happy preparations, you just stand silently and watch what seems like the *entire* world gear up for a fabulous party that you haven't been invited to.

Balls, is what it is. Just *balls*.

So what do you do? My first instinct when faced with adversity is to hide. Lock myself in and give up showering and burrow into my couch armed with chips and the Internet. Screw you, world! I don't need you! I have celebrity gossip and salty snacks!

This, however, is a foolish approach. And you risk looking like a fool if you adopt it, to say nothing of the fact that you will wake up the next day feeling useless and achy from inaction, bloated from all the fat and salt and tears.

What I propose is that, instead of turning inwards, you give outwards. The best way to instantly improve your mood and decrease holiday rage is to give back to your community.

Soup kitchens, homeless shelters, youth centers, senior homes—these are all places that could use a helping hand putting on holiday celebrations, whether it's a Christmas party or Thanksgiving feast, Valentine's Day dance or Festival of Lights. Get off your couch, make a few phone calls, and offer your help.

THE BENEFITS OF THIS ARE THREEFOLD.

1. Kind of like working out, no matter how reluctant or hesitant or completely, stubbornly unwilling you are to show up in the first place, you will feel *incredible* afterwards. You are helping people, and we humans

absolutely need to feel useful and helpful and *necessary.* This feeling beats sadness and beats anger, and it does a lot to make a dent in even the darkest depression.

2. It gives you some perspective. Nothing makes me feel like a bigger idiot than spending days (or, more embarrassingly accurate, *weeks*) feeling sorry for myself and then taking my head out of my butt and realizing that I really do have it good. *Really good*. Taking the time to help those less fortunate casts your own life in a new light. No, you might not have a partner on Valentine's Day but you have a home. Yes, you might be spending Christmas alone when everyone around you is enveloped into a happy crush of family and gifts, but you are healthy and able-bodied and that belly you hate when you look in the mirror every morning fills out that Santa suit perfectly. Listen to those who thank you for your service, and then look inside yourself and give thanks for what matters in your own life.

3. Of course, most importantly, you are helping those who need it. You are giving something without expecting anything in return, and I think that is the message at the core of most holidays, or it was until it got buried under an overdose of consumerism and unrealistic expectations. Being in a position to help others is one of the best feelings you can have, and you deserve that feeling. (You really do).

Holidays are a dark time for many of us. They can be incredibly gratifying but also profoundly isolating. Choosing to make a difference is truly the best gift you can give, to others and to yourself.

But wait! Don't think you're off the hook just because you love Valentine's Day and start humming Christmas carols in November. This practice of giving *out* instead of giving up or giving in isn't limited exclusively to the hermits and malcontents among us, it can be a great tradition to start within your own happy family.

To take the stress off of cooking a Thanksgiving dinner for twenty-one people, why not take the family to help serve others instead? Or, rather than buying gifts at Christmas, take your children to pick out gifts for less fortunate kids, or help them choose some of their gently used toys to give away.

At this point you may well be asking yourself, "This is all well and good, but why is it here? How is this green? How does any of this do-gooding end up being environmentally friendly?"

Well, aside from the fact that turning the spotlight away from buying and toward *doing* is imperative if we want to reduce both holiday consumption and holiday waste, it is also a simple exercise in the effect one individual can have on the world.

Social problems, like environmental problems, can seem overwhelming. Homelessness, addiction, global warming, suicide, and islands of garbage the size of Texas—these are Big Issues. They are scary and daunting and seemingly impervious to simple solutions. What can you, one person, do in the face of these Big Issues? What effect can one person have?

Honestly, not much. One person recycling when everyone else chooses not to doesn't objectively have much of an impact, but what happens when it is one *million* individuals, all feeling the same powerlessness? If each individual makes the decision to enact positive changes—however small—together these choices add up to a swelling cumulative change that could alter the landscape of our world forever.

It only takes one person to start, and you can only change your own behavior. This is true in relationships, and it is true when you begin to try to tackle those Big Issues. Listen to dear old Gandhi on this one, and be the change you want to see in the world.

Reduce, reuse, recycle, and choose to give *out* instead of giving up.

CONCLUSION

(OR: TIME TO PONY UP, FREELOADERS)

All right, I've now spent hundreds of pages detailing each and every one of my strange endeavors to reduce our environmental impact, from washing my hair with baking soda to keeping vegetable scraps in my freezer. I have laid it all on the table, I have given and given and given again, and now it's time for all you freeloaders to pony up and return the favor.

Your job, now that you know all these strange secrets, is to make me look less crazy. A tall order, I know, but I am asking nonetheless.

I keep dreaming about the day that I can walk into a coffee shop, place my order, and have the barista say, smiling "Oh! You've brought your own jar! Terrific."

I long for the afternoon that I suddenly notice, in the midst of dragging Gus around on his daily walk, that every backyard boasts a clothesline fluttering in the breeze, like little bunting banners made up of socks and underwear.

Also, I think I might just pee a little from excitement if I ever walk through a grocery store and see our favorite unassuming superstars, washing soda and borax, occupying prime retail space at eye level on the shelf.

Each time one of you adopts even a few of these little changes, I look less crazy. So if you won't do it for Al Gore, or the whales, or the children (*think of the children!*), will you do it for me?

The key here is to start slow and just keep going.

Now is not the time to tear through your home throwing out all your cleaners and toothpaste, making a complete 180 from your old life and driving your family mad. Take it easy, and adopt small changes as you go along. When you run out of glass cleaner, fill the bottle with vinegar and water instead. When you use the last bit of toothpaste, recycle the tube with Terracycle and make a little batch of your own.

If you go cold turkey, if you attempt to do too much, too soon, it will become horrible and overwhelming, you will become consumed with guilt and stress, and your partner will find you hiding under your dining room table with a white-knuckled grip on a secret stash of paper towels, rambling about coconut oil.

Obviously I've tried to write this book in a lighthearted and humorous way to make it enjoyable to read, but by taking this approach I don't mean to make light of the very real challenges we face when speaking about the devastating toll our actions are taking on this dear planet of ours.

I have tried to avoid using guilt-inducing scare tactics and shaming statistics because I do not believe that people become motivated by guilt, I believe they become immobilized by it. Sometimes, in our efforts to hammer home the gravity of the problem we currently face, we run the risk of becoming overwhelmed and sticking our heads in the sand, frightened into inaction.

But we do need to keep our heads up and pay attention, because what is at stake here is far greater than the cumulative millions of tons of waste we ship to the landfill each day. At stake is a fundamentally flawed way of thinking that has permeated almost every aspect of our society, from how we choose our cleaning supplies to how we choose our relationships.

We are filled with a desperate need to trade up, to discard the old and the familiar in favor of NEW! and IMPROVED!, in favor of products in shiny packaging that promise to solve all our problems—even the ones we didn't know we had.

Stop choosing disposable. Don't choose disposable forks and don't choose disposable people—both are flimsy and unreliable, and won't be in your life for the long haul. You deserve quality, both in the items you use in your daily life and in the people you share that life with.

Stop replacing, and start fixing. Choose something solid that can be maintained over time, or simply choose to not choose anything at all, and sit with that feeling of wanting, rather than rushing immediately to satiate it.

Above all, remember the Tao of the lazy environmentalist.

Namaste (only partially kidding),
Madeleine

ACKNOWLEDGEMENTS

First and foremost, my sincerest thanks go to Brenda Knight, who discovered this book hiding within the ten bulleted points of a small list. Without her this book wouldn't be here, and I wouldn't be able to end every argument with "To heck with you! I am a *published author,* dammit!" Thank you, Brenda (and sorry, everyone else). Thank you to everyone at Viva Editions for all of their hard work, including Kitty who edited this book and in doing so taught me many things, including the fact that it is "toward," not "towards."

I owe a huge debt of gratitude to my family (David, Jennifer, Liam, Kate, Lizzie, Claire, Darryl, Hilary, and Mawney Somerville) and Adam's family (Scott, Cathy, Christine, Chuck, Leigh and Rachid), who patiently saw me through every step of this journey. They tested recipes, watched Olive while I wrote, endured long-suffering sighs, and held their tongues when I refused to share even one word of the finished product with them before it was published.

Thank you to my friends who listened to me agonize and dither and procrastinate and stress. Your patience is endless, and your encouragement kept me going.

To the eleven or so readers of my blog, thank you for listening to me. Thank you for being a kind audience while I honed my voice and polished my words. And extra-special thanks to Ashley Austrew, Sara Lowe, Sarah Lebrun, and Valerie Beijos.

Incredible amounts of gratitude go to my daughter, Olive, for taking long naps so Mama could get some work done. She won't remember much of the writing that so consumed her early days, but she will grow up under this crazy hippie regime so I thank her in advance for her patience. Most of all, I beg her not to rebel against my teachings and end up living in a McMansion without a recycling bin, clad head-to-toe in parabens.

Finally, to Adam Greiner—the man, the muse, the dance moves. Thank you for always letting me exploit your antics for my own advancement, and also for holding my hand during this entire process. We met when I was eighteen, and you've loved me every day since. Without you, life would be very clean and very organized and very, *very* boring. I love you, indubitably.

NOTES

1. http://www.cbsnews.com/stories/2000/12/26/48hours/main259812.shtml
2. http://www.davidsuzuki.org/what-you-can-do/queen-of-green/faqs/cleaning/can-indoor-plants-improve-air-quality-inside-my-home/?gclid=CP6Mwumh4LYCFaaDQgodnBUA7w
3. http://preventdisease.com/news/articles/sex_makes_you_look_younger.shtml
4. http://www.levysmiles.com/docs/Abrasiveness_of_Common_Tooth-pase.pdf
5. http://www.sevencircles.org/Newsletter-Ceremony-MoonTime.html
6. http://www.nytimes.com/2013/03/10/opinion/sunday/living-with-less-a-lot-less.html?pagewanted=all&_r=0
7. Ibid.
8. http://www.epa.gov/greenhomes/ConserveWater.htm
9. http://enviroworld.ca/environmental-products/freegarden-rain
10. http://news.ca.msn.com/world/cbc-article.aspx?cp-documentid=253402484
11. http://www.time.com/time/health/article/0,8599,1880145,00.html
12. http://www.westcoastseeds.com/topicdetail/topic/companion-planting/
13. http://en.wikipedia.org/wiki/List_of_companion_plants
14. http://www.readersdigest.ca/health/healthy-living/bottled-water-vs-tap-water-rethink-what-you-drink

15. http://www.psychologytoday.com/blog/brain-sense/201201/the-placebo-effect-how-it-works
16. Graff, D., *Research on Mineral Absorption*, Weber State University, International Conference on Human Nutrition, 1995.
17. Lekovic, Jill M., *Diaper-Free Before 3* (New York: Harmony Books), 2006.

ABOUT THE AUTHOR

MADELEINE SOMERVILLE is thirty years old and often finds herself wondering how in the world that happened, exactly.

Her love of writing comes first, followed by an insatiable desire to create a simple, earth-friendly life. She finds herself inspired to create rather than consume, and enjoys tinkering with recipes for eco-friendly cleaning products and beauty fixes, along with trying to find ways to live happily with less.

She has a degree in sociology with a concentration in criminology, deviance, and social control, and a baby tooth. She once spent three terrifying minutes with a 200 pound albino python wrapped around her neck, and in 2009, her local paper ran an article shaming her for eating (and thoroughly enjoying) nachos from 7-Eleven.

She has never gone skydiving or bungee jumping and never will.

Madeleine lives in British Columbia, Canada with her daughter, her dog, and her husband, whom she once called "Couch Satan." She writes at SweetMadeleine.ca.

This is her first book.

Photograph by Adam Greiner.

INDEX

Abeego 125
acupuncture 182
Adam xviii, 11, 12, 33, 44, 47, 48, 58, 79, 85, 88, 92, 99, 155, 156
addiction 88–91, 252
all-purpose cleaner 20
aloe vera 66, 67, 221, 222
alternatives to dryer sheets 15
apple cider vinegar 54, 56, 60, 179, 180, 230
arrowroot powder 59
Ayurveda 184
baby xx, 94, 108, 193, 195–199, 201, 204–208, 210–215, 217–223, 232
baby wipe solution 221
baby wipes 218, 219
baking soda 13–15, 21, 24, 25, 34, 50, 51, 54, 56–59, 72, 169, 180, 228
beauty 43–45, 47, 50, 51, 60, 66, 118, 214, 263
belly butter 215, 217
boho table settings 120
borax xix, 13, 14, 20, 164, 255
Castile soap 20, 21, 27, 219–221, 239
cats 37, 231, 235
cloth diapers 183, 210–212
cloth wipes 219–221
clothesline 91, 92, 94, 96, 169, 255
coconut oil 46–49, 52, 59, 60, 68, 175, 192, 214, 217, 218, 223, 256
communal property 81
companion planting 134, 136, 141, 142
compost 4, 138, 140, 145–149, 156–160, 238, 239
consumption 4, 73, 83, 90, 115, 193, 204, 252
Craigslist 11, 196, 197
deodorant 59
depilatory cream 68
diamonds 66, 171, 172
diaper rash cream 223
disposable wipes 219
dogs xix, 11, 27, 30, 32, 35, 72, 79, 225–229, 232
Epsom salts 189–191
essential oils 17, 18, 41, 52, 57, 88, 98, 164, 177, 190, 191, 214, 215, 218, 228
Etsy 2, 18, 64, 66, 221
exercise 44, 128, 252
eye makeup remover 46
Facebook 11, 88, 197
family 74, 82, 122, 130, 147, 157, 195, 200, 221, 226, 232, 241, 244, 248, 249
farmers market xxi, 100, 111, 116, 118, 119, 130
feminism 64
flea spray 230
floor cleaner 26
floor duster 29
gender 171, 205, 206
gifts 170, 173, 174, 195, 241, 242–246, 248, 251, 252
Gitelman Syndrome 189
guilt xv–xvii, xx, 35, 90, 91, 101, 159, 163–165, 210, 234, 241, 256
Gus xix, 6, 11, 29, 30, 79, 80, 169, 179, 225–229, 231, 232, 234, 255
hands-free silver polish 23
hardwood floor polish 28, 76
herb garden 129, 132
hippies xvii, xviii, 18, 43, 53, 62, 95, 109, 134, 153, 157, 166, 170, 175, 182
home xiii, 1, 5, 40, 49, 74–79, 87, 94–96, 102, 121, 123, 129, 130
jewelry 24, 170, 171, 172

laundry detergent 13, 15, 40, 164, 212
lemon juice 52, 61, 69
litter boxes 231–234, 236, 239
magic tea 186–188
magnesium 189
makeup xv, 43–46, 164
man colds 186, 187
marriage 48, 167
massage oil 176
menstruation 61–65
meringue mask 60
minimalism 75, 113, 196
moisturizer 42, 47, 48, 51, 214, 218
Mother Nature xviii, 4, 43, 106, 150, 153, 159
moving 78, 98, 120
natural microdermabrasion 49, 50
neti pot 184–186
newspaper kitty litter 236
Olive xix, xx, 197, 198, 199, 204, 207, 208, 259
olive oil xvi, 27, 31, 32, 41, 52, 57, 131, 175, 219–222
organic xv, 51, 93, 115–118, 135, 141, 143, 145, 147, 164, 195
parabens 174, 217, 260
personal lubricant 174
pesticide-free garden 139, 141, 195
pesticides 137, 139, 141, 151, 195
pet bed 228, 229
pet toothpaste 230
Pinterest 89, 139
placebo 181, 182, 217
plants 31, 75, 95, 116, 119, 128–132, 134–144, 147, 149, 152, 153
plastic 6–9, 14, 17, 34–37, 40, 41, 45, 64–66, 68, 72, 85–87
possessions xvi, 2, 4, 5, 74, 79, 80, 82, 83, 168, 170
potty training 213
pregnancy xx, 193–196, 199, 211, 215, 217
punch-yourself-in-the-face salsa 111
rain barrel 95–97
raised garden beds 136, 138, 140
real live vegetable garden 132, 135
recycled paper gift bow 247
recycling xv, xviii, 1–4, 7, 18, 45, 46, 73, 84, 107, 116, 124, 156–161
reducing xviii, 2, 7, 17, 18, 34, 78, 102, 104, 107, 120, 123, 128, 146, 170
relationships xviii, 79, 155, 163, 166–171, 253, 257
reusable bags xvi, 85, 87, 102, 103, 161
reusing xviii, 2, 3, 18, 122
salad garden 131, 132
secondhand shopping 8–11, 66, 109, 115, 121–123, 196, 197, 199, 200, 210, 212, 213
seed storing 143
sesame oil 48, 51, 52, 177, 228
shampoo and conditioner 53, 54
shaving cream 40, 67, 68
shedding 11, 232
shopping 2, 4, 6, 8, 10, 11, 78, 86, 87, 89, 90, 100, 103, 104, 119
simple body scrubs 50, 51
soap 13, 14, 20–22, 26, 27, 31, 32, 37, 39–42, 49, 67, 123, 157
soap scum remover 22
sodium lauryl sulfate 54, 58
stainless-steel appliance cleaner 31
stainless-steel pots and pans polish 33
stinky dog spray 228
sustainability xiii, xiv, 65, 116, 162, 187, 203, 204, 226
take-out 105, 108, 109
Terracycle 45, 46, 59, 84, 256
toner 60, 112, 180
toothpaste 46, 57, 58, 230, 256
toys 84, 108, 195, 201–203, 225–227, 244, 252
toxins xv, xix, 17, 21, 45, 54, 69, 152, 160, 201, 203, 217
travel mugs 90, 107

triclosan 40, 41
tub scrub 21
tzatziki 104, 112
vermiculture 147
washing soda 13–15, 164, 255
waxing 68
weed barrier 138, 152, 153
weed killer 150
wheat kitty litter 235, 238
whipped body oil 49
white vinegar 20, 22, 29, 183, 239
window spray 29
worm compost 146, 147, 156
wrapping paper 118, 242, 243, 245
zero-electricity cold brewed coffee 113